THE HAGUE AND HAGUE-VISBY RULES

FOURTH EDITION

THE HAGUE AND HAGUE-VISBY RULES

by

JOHN RICHARDSON, FCII

FOURTH EDITION

|L|L|P|

LONDON   HONG KONG
1998

LLP Reference Publishing
69–77 Paul Street
London EC2A 4LQ
Great Britain

SOUTH EAST ASIA
LLP Asia Limited
Room 1101, Hollywood Centre
233 Hollywood Road
Hong Kong

First published in Great Britain 1985
Second edition 1989
Third edition 1994
Fourth edition 1998
© John Richardson 1985, 1989, 1994, 1998

British Library Cataloguing in Publication Data
A catalogue record
for this book is available
from the British Library

ISBN 1 85978 180 2

Are you satisfied with our customer service?

These telephone numbers are your service hot lines for questions and queries:

Delivery:	+44 (0) 1206 772866
Payment/invoices/renewals:	+44 (0) 1206 772114
LLP Products & Services:	+44 (0) 1206 772113

e-mail: Publications@LLPLimited.com or fax us on +44 (0) 1206 772771

*We welcome your views and comments in order to ease any problems
and answer any queries you may have.*

LLP Limited, Colchester CO3 3LP, U.K.

Text set in 10/12 Plantin by
Interactive Sciences Ltd
Gloucester
Printed in Great Britain by
WBC Limited
Bridgend, Mid-Glamorgan

ABOUT THE AUTHOR

JOHN RICHARDSON, F.C.I.I., is the risk analyst of P & O Nedlloyd Ltd. He has been involved in the development of the liability content of consortium operational contracts since the company commenced operating in 1969.

CONTENTS

TABLE OF CASES

INTRODUCTION

This book does not set out to challenge the authoritative works of Carver, Scrutton, Tetley and others on this subject, rather does it seek to provide, in digestible form for students and practitioners, a broad explanation of the operation of these Rules. Essentially the explanation will be of the interpretation of the Rules in English courts in the form of the Carriage of Goods by Sea Acts 1924 (Hague Rules) and 1971 (Hague-Visby Rules), both of which are reproduced in full in Appendix I (see pages 83 *et seq.*) with a cross reference to direct readers to comment on each section, Article or Rule thereof. However, as the application of the Rules is international, it is inevitable that references will be made in passing to the interpretation of certain foreign courts to some of the Rules' provisions.

As nations adopted the Rules, many made alterations to the text of the International Conventions, particularly in the case of the Hague Rules and especially to Article IV, Rule 5, and Article IX of these Rules. Therefore, it is necessary to study the relevant Act of each country before coming to any conclusions as to the effect of the Rules in that country. Fortunately, the UK Act differs little from the International Convention. Where it does so, this will be indicated.

Due to the international "broad brush" approach, whilst reference will be made to certain leading cases, no attempt will be made to provide an exhaustive list of cases, which is better left to the more authoritative works of reference on this subject mentioned earlier.

As the Hague and Hague-Visby Rules are identical for the larger part of their text, it is intended to offer the guide in a joint form highlighting where the differences occur and the effects of them. In this way, it is hoped to provide readers with a broad understanding of the provisions of both sets of Rules as interpreted through the English courts. However, as the preambles and introductory clauses to the Acts are quite different, they are dealt with separately at the beginning.

The correct title of what is better known as the Hague Rules is: "The International Convention for the Unification of Certain Rules relating to Bills of Lading signed at Brussels on 25th August 1924". These Rules, slightly amended, form the Schedule to the United Kingdom Carriage of Goods by Sea Act (COGSA) 1924.

The Hague-Visby Rules consist of the original Hague Rules amended by what are called the Visby Amendments but are more properly referred to as "The Protocol to amend the International Convention for the Unification of Certain Rules of Law relating to Bills of Lading signed at Brussels on 25th August 1924—Brussels 23rd February 1968". COGSA 1971 applies the original Hague Rules incorporating those amendments set out in the Visby Amendments (to produce what has become known as the Hague-Visby Rules) as the Schedule to that Act.

The Protocol was not a revised set of Rules, but an agreed set of instructions to convert the existing Hague Rules into the new Hague-Visby Rules; a "conversion kit".

Whilst it is generally well known how the Hague Rules came to be so called, the origin of Visby is not so generally appreciated and the story thereof makes amusing reading. Visby is the capital of the Swedish island and administrative district of Gotland in the Baltic Sea. An ancient port, it became, in the 13th century, the centre of the mercantile association which monopolised the Baltic trade and extended its operations eastward to Novgorod and westward to England. Later the Visby association was absorbed into the Hanseatic League, of which Visby became an important member. Visby gave its name to the Laws of Visby, a maritime legal code. It was a happy conceit of the CMI's Sub-Committee on Bill of Lading clauses that the name of Visby became associated with the proposed amendments to the Hague Rules. In their report of March 1962 (made with a view to the forthcoming CMI Conference in Stockholm in 1963) the Sub-Committee reported that:

"The members were much attracted by a proposal that, should the 'Positive Recommendations' be adopted . . . at the 1963 Conference, it might be possible for the Chairman of the CMI, the Secretaries General and those members of the CMI who so desire to take the plane from Stockholm to the Island of Gotland in the Baltic (a trip of one hour) and sign the recommendations in the old and beautiful city of Visby. The recommendations would then be known as the Visby Rules, thus forging a link with the Visby Sealaw of Mediaeval times. Perhaps the sense of tradition to which this name appeals might make the innovations of the Sub-Committee easier to accept. The whole set of Rules in respect of Bills of Lading sponsored by the CMI might in this way become known as the 'Hague-Visby Rules'."

The above rites were duly performed, but the recommendations signed at Visby were later much amended in the course of the Diplomatic Conference in Brussels in 1967 and 1968.

The updating of this fourth edition of this book has been deliberately delayed until after the 1997 CMI Centenary meeting in Antwerp, at which the subject of carriers' liabilities was on the agenda, so that any decisions taken in that forum could be reflected in the redraft. In fact, despite much debate, no developments of any significance emerged. This will almost certainly mean that the US and Australia in particular will proceed with their individual plans to produce domestic legislation of their own, based on the Hague-Visby Rules but with substantial deviations therefrom, which will only exacerbate the drift away from international uniformity in the Rules governing international carriage of goods by sea. For this reason a new Part has been added outlining current developments in legislation governing the carriage of goods by sea where the law is Hague/Hague-Visby based but has deviated from the strict Hague/Hague-Visby approach.

The opportunity has also been taken to update the York-Antwerp Rules to the current 1994 version (which replaced the 1974 version following the CMI meeting in Sydney in 1994) and to provide a specimen copy of the 1995 Lloyd's Salvage Agreement, LOF 1995. Also updated is the list of nations applying the Rules, most of whom have ratified or acceded to the Rules but several of whom have merely applied them by domestic legislation, which is much more difficult to keep track of as no centralised records are made of such arrangements. Details are also added of the 1996 Protocol on Limitation of Liability agreed at the London Convention in April/May 1996, which is likely to come into effect in the next few years and the CMI Uniform Rules for Sea Waybills and Rules for Electronic Bills of Lading as both of these promise to become of increasing importance in the future.

I trust that readers will find this expanded fourth edition of increased use as a guide and work of reference.

September 1997   JOHN RICHARDSON

PART 1

PREAMBLES AND INTRODUCTORY CLAUSES

Whilst the Rules which form the Schedules to COGSA 1924 (Hague Rules) and COGSA 1971 (Hague-Visby Rules) have a common base and lend themselves to a comparative study, the preambles and introductory clauses of the two Acts are substantially different and require separate study.

1924 ACT (COGSA)

This Act, which is described as:

"CARRIAGE OF GOODS BY SEA ACT 1924
An Act to amend the law with respect to the carriage of goods by sea. [1st August, 1924]"

has the following preamble:

"Whereas at the International Conference on Maritime Law held at Brussels in October, 1922, the delegates at the Conference, including the delegates representing His Majesty, agreed unanimously to recommend their respective Governments to adopt as the basis of a convention a draft convention for the unification of certain rules relating to bills of lading:
And whereas at a meeting held at Brussels in October, 1923, the rules contained in the said draft convention were amended by the Committee appointed by the said Conference:
And whereas it is expedient that the said rules as so amended and as set out with modifications in the Schedule to this Act (in this Act referred to as 'the Rules') should, subject to the provisions of this Act, be given the force of law with a view to establishing the responsibilities, liabilities, rights and immunities attaching to carriers under bills of lading:
Be it therefore enacted by the King's most Excellent Majesty, by and with the advice and consent of the Lords Spiritual and Temporal, and Commons, in this present Parliament assembled, and by the authority of the same, as follows:—"

Beyond giving a brief historical insight into the circumstances in which the Rules were drafted and adopted, the Preamble tells us little or nothing of significance and it is noticeable that the 1971 Act Preamble is reduced down to the obligatory preamble contained in the last paragraph of the 1924 Act.

1

On the other hand, the introductory clauses are important and have total control of how and when the Rules will be applied. Accordingly, they warrant closer study than they are often afforded.

Section 1

Section 1 reads:

"Subject to the provisions of this Act, the Rules shall have effect in relation to and in connection with the carriage of goods by sea in ships carrying goods from any port in Great Britain or Northern Ireland to any other port whether in or outside Great Britain or Northern Ireland."

and needs to be read in conjunction with Section 4, which reads:

"Article VI of the Rules shall, in relation to the carriage of goods by sea in ships carrying goods from any port in Great Britain or Northern Ireland to any other port in Great Britain or Northern Ireland or to a port in the Irish Free State, have effect as though the said Article referred to goods of any class instead of to particular goods and as though the proviso to the second paragraph of the said Article were omitted."

Section 1 provides for the Rules to apply to shipment of goods from all ports in Great Britain or Northern Ireland. Note that the Rules are applied to exports only and not imports. This is not entirely in accordance with the intentions of the drafters, which have generally not been respected, many states having followed the UK lead of applying the Rules on the basis of the port of shipment rather than place of issue of the bill of lading (*see* Article X of the Rules, page 54). In the case of the US COGSA 1936 it is applied to imports as well as exports.

By widening the categories of goods to which Article VI applies to cover all goods when shipment is to another port in Great Britain, Northern Ireland or the Republic of Ireland, section 4 effectively qualifies section 1 to remove from the scope of the Act all goods moving coastwise or across the Irish Sea.

Thus the 1924 Act applies to exports only from ports in Great Britain or Northern Ireland to ports outside Great Britain, Northern Ireland or the Republic of Ireland.

The equivalent section in the 1971 Act is section 1(3) which makes the provisions of the Act applicable to all shipments from UK ports, whether international or not, so that coastal trade now comes within the scope of the Act. However, it must be remembered that the Acts govern only shipments covered by "Bills of Lading or similar documents of title" (*see* section 3) and, if none are issued, the Acts cannot apply. Thus coastal and short sea operators, seeking to avoid the application of the Acts, can do so if they can persuade their customers to forgo their right to demand a bill of lading (*see* Article III, Rule 3, page 22) and instead accept a consignment note, non-negotiable receipt or some other document which is neither a bill of lading nor a document of title. This approach is much favoured by many coastal and short sea operators and even deep-sea operators have been known to attempt to apply it.

Section 2

Section 2 reads:

"There shall not be implied in any contract for the carriage of goods by sea to which the Rules apply any absolute undertaking by the carrier of the goods to provide a seaworthy ship."

and relieves the carrier of any absolute warranty of seaworthiness. This is replaced by the Article III, Rule 1, requirement to exercise due diligence (*see* page 19). This point is covered in section 3 of the 1971 Act where, except for a minor drafting change, it is repeated, so that there is no difference between the 1924 and 1971 Acts on this account. (This point will be discussed in greater detail when considering Article III, Rule 1, page 19).

Section 3

Section 3 is known as the "Clause Paramount requirement" and reads:

"Every bill of lading, or similar document of title, issued in Great Britain or Northern Ireland which contains or is evidence of any contract to which the Rules apply shall contain an express statement that it is to have effect to the provisions of the said Rules as applied by this Act."

The reason for this is that the Act will not be mandatory law in the court of a foreign country to which the ship may travel, so that the only way to ensure its application is by contractual incorporation. In any event, it may happen that the importing country will have overriding legislation—e.g. the USA will apply their 1936 Act to imports as well as exports and thereby apply their limit of liability, US$500 per package or customary freight unit instead of the UK limit of £100 per package (note difference in basis as well as amount). Furthermore, the clause is a "paper tiger" as there is no prescribed penalty for non-compliance, so that this section is frequently ignored with impunity, unlike in the USA, where failure to comply means the shipowner being deprived of limitation if brought before a US court. There is no equivalent section in the 1971 Act, but Article IV *bis*, of the rules in the Schedule thereto provides for the Rules to apply in any action, whether in contract or in tort.

Section 4

See the notes on section 1.

Section 5

Section 5 of the 1924 Act gives the shipowner (carrier) protection when carrying bulk cargoes, for which he is required by custom of the trade to issue a bill of lading for weight, which he has no accurate means of checking, by providing that the weight shown in such circumstances is not *prima facie* evidence against him. The shipper also enjoys similar protection. This modifies Article III, Rules 4 and 5 of the Schedule.

This concession has been withdrawn in the 1971 Act, which incorporates no such provision. In the 1924 Act it reads as follows:

"Where under the custom of any trade the weight of any bulk cargo inserted in the bill of lading is a weight ascertained or accepted by a third party other than the carrier or the shipper and the fact that the weight is so ascertained or accepted is stated in the bill of lading, then, notwithstanding anything in the Rules, the bill of lading shall not be deemed to be *prima facie* evidence against the carrier of the receipt of goods of the weight so inserted in the bill of lading, and the accuracy thereof at the time of shipment shall not be deemed to have been guaranteed by the shipper."

Section 6

Section 6 has three subsections:

Subsection (1)

Subsection (1) provides the title by which the Act may be cited:

"This Act may be cited as the Carriage of Goods by Sea Act, 1924."

Subsection (2)

Subsection (2) reads as follows:

"Nothing in this Act shall effect the operation of sections four hundred and forty-six to four hundred and fifty, both inclusive, five hundred and two, and five hundred and three of the Merchant Shipping Act, 1894, as amended by any subsequent enactment, or the operation of any other enactment for the time being in force limiting the liability of the owners of seagoing vessels."

and retains the paramount effect of the Merchant Shipping Act (MSA) relating to the shipowner's right to limitation over the limitation provisions of the Rules. It is a duplication of Article VIII, more specifically expressed with reference to the relevant UK Act. Thus, if total claims against a ship calculated in accordance with the Rules exceed the limitation provided in the MSA, all claims are scaled down *pro rata* so that the total claims do not exceed the MSA limitation fund.

This provision always presupposes that the shipowner has complied with the provisions of the MSA necessary to qualify for limitation. These tend to differ from country to country because not all nations have ratified the Limitation of Shipowners Liability Convention signed in Brussels in October 1957, the USA being a prime example. Thus some nations apply the Limitation of Shipowners Liability Convention signed in Brussels in October 1957, some others apply the 1976 Convention on Limitation of Liability for Maritime Claims, whilst there are others (like the USA) who apply alternative bases.

Up to 1 December 1986 the 1957 Convention was the leading Convention. It was given the force of law in the United Kingdom by the Merchant Shipping

(Liability of Shipowners and Others) Act 1958 (an amending subsequent enactment to the MSA 1894) and permitted shipowners, charterers and ship managers to limit liability in accordance with the Act, unless they were guilty of actual fault or privity.

Limitation under the 1958 MSA used to be calculated in the fictitious currency of Poincaré francs in the same way as the Hague-Visby limit used to, and required Orders in Council to translate it into sterling equivalents, but, with effect from 29 November 1984 the 1979 Special Drawing Rights (SDR) Protocol was applied to MSA limits producing the figures below. SDRs are a mean of a basket of international currencies, readily convertible into any required currency from regular details available in the financial press, thus obviating the need for continual Orders in Council for translation into meaningful currency.

In respect of loss of life and/or personal injury claims only, there is a minimum limitation tonnage of 300 to provide a reasonable fund for such claims on small vessels. Limitation tonnage is calculated by reference to the net registered tonnage of the vessel plus the amount deducted from the gross registered tonnage on account of engine room space.

The 1958 MSA (as amended by the appropriate SDR Protocol) provides the following basis of limitation:

(a) For loss of life and/or personal injury only including passengers— 206.67 SDRs per ton

(b) For damage to property only— 66.67 SDRs per ton

(c) For loss of life and/or personal injury and damage— 206.67 SDRs per ton
to property in . . . case the first 140 SDRs per ton are applied to loss of life and/or personal injury claims only and, to the extent that these are not satisfied by the limitation fund of 140 SDRs per ton, the balance of such claims rank *pari passu* (on equal terms) with the property claims for the remaining 66.67 SDRs per ton. Thus if personal injury claims were less than the 140 SDRs fund, the shipowner would pay them in full and invoke limitation only against the property claims as per (b) above.

In the UK, courts have generally been reluctant to break limitation, except in clearly defined cases of fault and privity of the shipowner or his alter ego, and the benefit of limitation extends to charterers and ship managers as well as shipowners. This is by no means a universal approach and in many jurisdictions charterers and ship managers find themselves unprotected and in need of the protection of a demise clause in the bill of lading (always assuming that the jurisdiction to which they are subjected recognises the validity of such clauses).

On 1 December 1986 the 1976 Convention on Limitation of Liability for Maritime Claims became operative. As at April 1997 the signatories applying this Convention were:

Australia	Egypt	Liberia	Sweden
Bahamas	Equatorial Guinea	Marshall Islands	Switzerland
Barbados	Finland	Mexico	United Kingdom
Belgium	France	Netherlands	Vanuatu
Belize	Germany	New Zealand	Yemen Arab Republic
Benin	Georgia	Norway	
Croatia	Greece	Poland	
Denmark	Japan	Spain	

N.B. China and South Korea have enacted legislation broadly in line with the 1976 Convention.

In the United Kingdom the enabling Act is the Merchant Shipping Act 1979.

This new Convention substantially increases the size of the limitation fund, but creates an almost unbreakable right to limit. Article 4 thereof provides as follows:

"A person liable shall not be entitled to limit his liability if it is proved that the loss resulted from his personal act or omission, committed with the intent to cause such loss, or recklessly and with knowledge that such would probably result".

Clearly this is a far more difficult requirement to overcome than "fault and privity".

The limits in the 1976 Convention are higher and rather more complex than those in the 1957 Convention and are as follows:

(a)   In respect of loss of life or personal injury (excluding passengers for whom a separate additional fund is created based on the number of passengers which the vessel is certificated to carry):
   (i)   333,000 units of account (SDR) for a ship with a tonnage not exceeding 500 tons.
   (ii)   For a ship with a tonnage in excess thereof, in addition:
      for each ton from 501 to 3,000 tons: 500 SDRs;
      for each ton from 3,001 to 30,000 tons: 333 SDRs;
      for each ton from 30,001 to 70,000 tons: 250 SDRs;
      for each ton in excess of 70,000 tons: 167 SDRs.
(b)   In respect of any other claims:
   (i)   167,000 SDRs for a ship not exceeding 500 tons.
   (ii)   For a ship with a tonnage in excess thereof, in addition:

for each ton from 501 to 30,000 tons: 167 SRDs;
for each ton from 30,001 to 70,000 tons: 125 SDRs;
for each ton in excess of 70,000 tons: 83 SDRs.

(Note that minimum limitation tonnage is now increased to 500 and limitation tonnage is calculated according to the 1969 International Convention on Tonnage Measurement of Ships.)

The SDR is to be converted into national currency according to the methods of the International Monetary Fund. If a state is not a member of that Fund, the values set out in SDRs are expressed in monetary units of 65.5 milligrams of gold in millesimal fineness nine hundred (i.e. Poincaré francs) which are to be converted into national currency according to the law of the state concerned.

As with the 1957 Convention, the balances of unsatisfied loss of life or personal injury claims (a) can participate *pari passu* along with the other claims (b). Accordingly, total limitation where loss of life and/or personal injury claims are involved in conjunction with other claims is found by adding the amounts produced by formulae (a) and (b) together.

At an international conference on Hazardous and Noxious Substances and Limitation of Liability hosted by the International Maritime Organisation (IMO) in London in April/May 1996, a Protocol was agreed to amend the limits in the 1976 Convention. It will enter into force 90 days after the 10th state expresses consent to be bound by it, which is expected to take approximately three years. The United Kingdom will be amongst the 10 inaugural states to apply this Protocol.

The increase is greatest for small ships as the minimum tonnage is increased from 500 to 2,000. The new limits are:

    (a)   in respect of claims for loss of life or personal injury:
           (i) 2 million SDRs for a ship with a tonnage not exceeding 2,000 tons,
         (ii) for a ship with a tonnage in excess thereof, the following amount in addition to that mentioned in (i);
               for each ton from 2,001 to 30,000 tons, 800 SDRs;
               for each ton from 30,001 to 70,000 tons, 600 SDRs;
               for each ton in excess of 70,000 tons, 400 SDRs.
    (b)   in respect of any other claims:
           (i) 1 million SDRs for a ship with a tonnage not exceeding 2,000 tons;
         (ii) for a ship with a tonnage in excess thereof the following amount in addition to that mentioned in (i);
               for each ton from 2,001 to 30,000 tons, 400 SDRs;
               for each ton from 30,001 to 70,000 tons, 300 SDRs; and
               for each ton in excess of 70,000 tons, 200 SDRs.

Similar arrangements to those made under the 1976 Convention apply for states that are not members of the International Monetary Fund.

Alternative bases of limitation are used in some jurisdictions, a favourite being the value of the ship plus freight, which basis applies in the USA. If limitation arises in a situation where a vessel has sunk (say due to a collision) this produces a very inadequate fund, so that US courts are very receptive to the proposals of plaintiffs to deny limitation to shipowners on account of fault and privity, often on the most obscure grounds.

This important provision of the 1924 Act is, in fact, a reinforcement of a point covered in the Rules as Article VIII, which only serves to emphasise the importance which Parliament placed upon this provision, in that they felt obliged to duplicate the provisions of the Rules in their own drafting of introductory clauses. It should be noted, however, that in both cases in the 1924 Act reference is made to shipowners only, with no mention of "others". The 1958 MSA was in operation by the time of the 1971 Act, so the equivalent section in the 1971 Act (s. 6(4)) makes reference to "shipowners and others" in the style of 1958 MSA.

Subsection (3)

Section 6(3) reads:

"The Rules shall not by virtue of this Act apply to any contract for the carriage of goods by sea made before such day, not being earlier than the thirtieth day of June, nineteen hundred and twenty-four, as His Majesty may by Order in Council direct, nor to any bill of lading or similar document of title issued, whether before or after such day as aforesaid, in pursuance of any such contract as aforesaid."

and provides a starting date for the 1924 Act.

1971 ACT (COGSA)

This Act is described as:

"CARRIAGE OF GOODS BY SEA ACT 1971
An Act to amend the law with respect to the carriage of goods by sea".

and is introduced only by the following obligatory brief preamble:

"Be it enacted by the Queen's most Excellent Majesty, by and with the advice and consent of the Lords Spiritual and Temporal, and Commons, in this present Parliament assembled, and by the authority of the same, as follows:—"

Section 1

Section 1 has seven subsections:

Subsection (1)

This is a definitions clause for the word "Rules" and initially read:

"In this Act, 'the Rules' means the International Convention for the unification of certain rules of law relating to bills of lading signed at Brussels on 25th August 1924, as amended by the Protocol signed at Brussels on 23rd February 1968."

Following the enactment of the Merchant Shipping Act 1981 the words:

"and by the Protocol signed at Brussels on 21st December 1979."

were added to provide reference to the Act which changed the limitation currency from Poincaré francs to Special Drawing Rights (SDRs)—*see* subsection (5), page 10, and Article IV, Rule 5(*a*), page 46.

Subsection (2)

Subsection (2) may be described as the "enacting clause", giving the Rules the force of law:

"The provisions of the Rules, as set out in the Schedule to this Act, shall have the force of law."

Subsection (3)

Subsection (3) is the equivalent of sections 1 and 4 of the 1924 Act and provides details of the scope of the 1971 Act thus:

"Without prejudice to subsection (2) above, the said provisions shall have effect (and have the force of law) in relation to and in connection with the carriage of goods by sea in ships where the port of shipment is a port in the United Kingdom, whether or not the carriage is between ports in two different States within the meaning of Article X of the Rules."

Notice the emphasis placed upon the fact that the Act applies to all shipments from UK ports, whether national or international in character. This contravenes Article X of the Rules, which provides for the Rules to apply only "to the carriage of goods between ports in two different States". As was previously noted when considering sections 1 and 4 of the 1924 Act (*see* page 2), this provision is frequently circumvented by avoiding the issue of a bill of lading or similar document of title, as the Rules are specified as applying as mandatory law only where such documents are issued. *See* subsection (4).

Subsection (4)

Subsection (4), which has to be read in conjunction with subsection (6), reads:

"Subject to subsection (6) below, nothing in this section shall be taken as applying anything in the Rules to any contract for the carriage of goods by sea, unless the contract expressly or by implication provides for the issue of a bill of lading or any similar document of title."

Subsection (6)

The qualifying subsection (6) provides:

"Without prejudice to Article X(c) of the Rules, the Rules shall have the force of law in relation to:—
  (*a*)   any bill of lading if the contract contained in or evidenced by it expressly provides that the Rules shall govern the contract, and
  (*b*)   any receipt which is a non-negotiable document marked as such if the contract contained in or evidenced by it is a contract for the carriage of goods by sea which expressly provides that the Rules are to govern the contract as if the receipt were a bill of lading,
but subject, where paragraph (*b*) applies, to any necessary modifications and in particular with the omission in Article III of the Rules of the second sentence of paragraph 4 and of paragraph 7."

Article X(*c*) provides for contractual application of the Hague-Visby Rules so subsection 6(*a*) is a reinforcement and qualification of that provision—(*see* discussion on Article X on page 54)—By making subsection (4) subject to subsection (6) and thus excluding occasions where the Rules are contractually incorporated, an exception is made to the general rule in subsection (4).

Subsection (6)(*b*) allows for contractual application where a non-negotiable document is issued instead of a "bill of lading or similar document of title". This is clearly to cover the growing use of waybills (which are receipts and contracts of carriage but not documents of title) as well as non-negotiable receipts (NNRs), Consignment Notes etc., which contractually incorporate the Hague-Visby Rules rather than use the opportunity to avoid them.

Where the Hague-Visby Rules are applied contractually in accordance with subsection (6)(*b*), the carrier is excused compliance with Article III, Rule 4, second sentence (which estops the carrier from pleading the defence of error in the bill of lading when transferred to a third party acting in good faith) and Rule 7 (the requirement to issue a bill of lading upon demand).

Subsection (5)

Subsection (5) reads as follows:

"The Secretary of State may from time to time by order made by statutory instrument specify the respective amounts which for the purposes of paragraph 5 of Article IV of the Rules and of Article IV *bis* of the Rules are to be taken as equivalent to the sums expressed in francs which are mentioned in sub-paragraph (*a*) of that paragraph."

and provides for the periodic issue of Orders in Council by the Secretary of State giving sterling equivalents to the limitations of liability in the Rules, which are expressed in Poincaré gold francs (Poincaré francs are defined in Article IV, Rule 5(*d*), *see* page 48), and, being a fictitious currency, do not have any ready source of exchange into international currencies. However, since February 1984, as a result of the coming into force the 1979 Hague-Visby Special Drawing Rights Protocol, the Hague-Visby Rules limitation has been changed to expression in Special Drawing Rights (SDRs) (a mean of a basket of international currencies, the exchange into international currencies of which is readily available from the financial press) in those nations that are signatories thereto. For signatories to the SDR Protocol *see* page 46.

Although the introduction of the SDR Protocol by the Merchant Shipping Act 1981 makes this subsection superfluous, it is still retained in the Act (*see* subsection (1), page 9, and Article IV, Rule 5(*a*), page 46).

Subsection (7)

Section 1 is concluded with subsection (7) which provides:

"If and so far as the contract contained in or evidenced by a bill of lading or receipt within paragraph (*a*) or (*b*) of subsection (6) above applies to deck cargo or live animals, the Rules as given the force of law by that subsection shall have effect as if Article 1(*c*) did not exclude deck cargo and live animals.

In this subsection 'deck cargo' means cargo which by the contract of carriage is stated as being carried on deck and is so carried."

This is a classic example of how the wording of the Act interferes with the intention of the Convention by overturning one of its provisions. In Article 1(*c*) of the Convention "Goods" are clearly defined for the purposes of the Convention as excluding live animals and deck cargo shipped against an appropriately claused bill, so that the Convention is not designed to apply to these categories of cargo. However, section 1(7) of the Act interferes with this arrangement by creating a situation where, if the carrier inserts an unqualified clause paramount (i.e. a clause whose provisions override all others and take paramount effect) in his bill to give contractual effect to the Act in any foreign court, which may override the jurisdiction clause and hear the case, he automatically undertakes to apply the Rules to live animals and deck cargo. Only by judiciously wording his clause paramount to exclude live animals and deck cargo from its influence may the carrier apply the intention of the Rules and carry live animals and deck cargo at merchant's risk.

It is, perhaps, significant that the 1971 Act has no equivalent to section 3 of the 1924 Act, which requires the insertion of a clause paramount in all relevant bills of lading, although it is mandatorily applied to tortious claims as well as contractual claims by Article IV *bis*.

Section 2

Section 2 reads as follows:

"(1) If Her Majesty by Order in Council certifies to the following effect, that is to say, that for the purposes of the Rules:
    (*a*) a State specified in the Order is a contracting State, or is a contracting State in respect of any place or territory so specified; or
    (*b*) any place or territory specified in the Order forms part of a State so specified (whether a contracting State or not),
the Order shall, except so far as it has been superseded by a subsequent Order, be conclusive evidence of the matters so certified.

(2) An Order in Council under this section may be varied or revoked by a subsequent Order in Council."

and is a purely administrative section which links with sections 4 and 5 to provide for the power of government to extend the application of the Act to colonies, dominions etc. by means of the Order in Council procedure.

Section 3

Section 3 which reads as follows:

"There shall not be implied in any contract for the carriage of goods by sea which the Rules apply by virtue of this Act any absolute undertaking by the carrier of the goods to provide a seaworthy ship."

is identical to section 2 of the 1924 Act, upon which comment has already been made (*see* page 3).

Sections 4 and 5

Sections 4 and 5 read as follows:

"**4.**—(1) Her Majesty may by Order in Council direct that this Act shall extend, subject to such exceptions, adaptations and modifications as may be specified in the Order, to all or any of the following territories, that is:—

> (a) any colony (not being a colony for whose external relations a country other than the United Kingdom is responsible),
> (b) any country outside Her Majesty's dominions in which Her Majesty has jurisdiction in right of Her Majesty's Government of the United Kingdom.

(2) An Order in Council under this section may contain such transitional and other consequential and incidental provisions as appear to Her Majesty to be expedient, including provisions amending or repealing any legislation about the carriage of goods by sea forming part of the law of any of the territories mentioned in paragraphs (a) and (b) above.

(3) An Order in Council under this section may be varied or revoked by a subsequent Order in Council.

5.—(1) Her Majesty may by Order in Council provide that section 1(3) of this Act shall have effect as if the reference therein to the United Kingdom included a reference to all or any of the following territories, that is:—

> (a) the Isle of Man;
> (b) any of the Channel Islands specified in the Order;
> (c) any colony specified in the Order (not being a colony for whose external relations a country other than the United Kingdom is responsible);
> (d) any associated state (as defined by section 1(3) of the West Indies Act 1967) specified in the Order;
> (e) any country specified in the Order, being a country outside Her Majesty's dominions in which Her Majesty has jurisdiction in right of Her Majesty's Government of the United Kingdom.

(2) An Order in Council under this section may be varied or revoked by a subsequent Order in Council."

(*See* Section 2 above for comment.)

Section 6

The final section of the Act is section 6, which has the following five sub-sections.

Subsection (1)

Like subsection 6(1) of the 1924 Act, subsection (1) provides the title by which the Act may be cited:

"This Act may be cited as the Carriage of Goods by Sea Act 1971."

Subsection (2)

Subsection (2) emphasises that the application of the Act extends to Northern Ireland:

"it is hereby declared that this Act extends to Northern Ireland."

Subsection (3)

Subsection (3) provides for repealing:

(a) COGSA 1924;
(b) reference to COGSA 1924 in the Nuclear Installations Act 1965 in section 12(4)(*a*) and in the Hovercraft Act 1968;

in order to prevent two conflicting Acts being on the statute book concurrently and to update cross-references to COGSA in associated Acts; thus:

"The following enactments shall be repealed, that is:
(*a*) the Carriage of Goods by Sea Act 1924,
(*b*) section 12(4)(*a*) of the Nuclear Installations Act 1965,
and without prejudice to section 38(1) of the Interpretation Act 1889, the reference to the said Act of 1924 in section 1(*1*)(i)(ii) of the Hovercraft Act 1968 shall include a reference to this Act."

Subsection (4)

Subsection (4) is a clear cross-reference linking Article VIII of the Rules with section 502 of the Merchant Shipping Act 1894 (as amended by the Merchant Shipping (Liability of Shipowners and others) Act 1958) to avoid any doubt that the statute envisaged in Article VIII of the Rules, so far as the UK is concerned, is the Merchant Shipping Act.

"It is hereby declared that for the purposes of Article VIII of the Rules section 502 of the Merchant Shipping Act 1894 (which, as amended by the Merchant Shipping (Liability of Shipowners and Others) Act 1958, entirely exempts shipowners and others in certain circumstances from liability for loss of, or damage to, goods) is a provision relating to limitation of liability."

Subsection (5)

Finally, subsection (5) provides for the Act to come into force by means of an Order in Council at some future date undetermined at the time of enactment.

"This Act shall come into force on such day as Her Majesty may by Order in Council appoint, and, for the purposes of the transition from the law in force immediately before the day appointed under this subsection to the provisions of this Act, the Order appointing the day may provide that those provisions shall have effect to such transitional provisions as may be contained in the Order."

This machinery was necessary because in 1971, at the time when this Act was passed by Parliament, an insufficient number of signatories had ratified or acceded to the Brussels Protocol of 1968, which required ratification or accession by 10 states, of which at least five were required to have over 1 million gross registered tons on their registry, whereupon it would come into force as an international Convention three months after the date of signature of the tenth state. On 23 March 1977 Ecuador acceded to the 1968 Protocol, so that it came into force as an International Convention on 23 June 1977. On 8 June 1977, by means of the COGSA 1971 (Commencement) Order 1977, COGSA 1971 was given the force of law in the UK with effect from 23 June 1977.

SCHEDULES TO THE ACTS (THE RULES)

Whereas it is necessary to deal with the introductory clauses to the 1924 and 1971 COGSA separately because they are so different, it is possible and desirable to deal with the Schedules to those Acts: the Hague Rules and Hague-Visby Rules, respectively, together, because they are identical in most areas and, where they differ, it is easier to highlight the differences by drawing direct comparisons. Except where stated, the Rules are identical, so remarks are equally applicable to both sets of Rules.

ARTICLE I: DEFINITIONS

The Rules start with five definitions to make clear the precise meaning of key words used in the Rules thus:

"In these Rules the following words are employed, with the meanings set out below:—

(a) 'Carrier' includes the owner or the charterer who enters into a contract of carriage with a shipper.

(b) 'Contract of carriage' applies only to contracts of carriage covered by a bill of lading or any similar document of title, in so far as such document relates to the carriage of goods by sea, including any bill of lading or any similar document as aforesaid issued under or pursuant to a charter party from the moment at which such a bill of lading or similar document of title regulates the relations between a carrier and a holder of the same.

(c) 'Goods' includes goods, wares, merchandise, and articles of every kind whatsoever except live animals and cargo which by the contract of carriage is stated as being carried on deck and is so carried.

(d) 'Ship' means any vessel used for the carriage of goods by sea.

(e) 'Carriage of goods' covers the period from the time when the goods are loaded on to the time they are discharged from the ship."

(a) "Carrier"

"(a) 'Carrier' includes the owner or the charterer who enters into a contract of carriage with a shipper."

"Carrier" is quite straightforward—the carrier is the party "who enters into a contract of carriage with the shipper". The problem here is to identify that party accurately from the contract of carriage issued. It is frequently not the party whose name or logo appears on the face of the contract and, in some cases, it is not possible positively to identify the carrier.

For example, the contract may contain a demise clause along the following lines:

"If the Ocean Vessel is not owned or chartered by demise to the Carrier issuing this Bill of Lading (as may be the case notwithstanding anything that appears to the contrary), then this Bill of Lading shall take effect only as a contract of Carriage between the Merchant and the owner or demise charterer (as the case may be) as principal through the agency of the named Carrier, who acts as agents only and shall be under no personal liability whatsoever in respect thereof."

in which case the carrier is the owner or demise charterer of the vessel. Lloyd's Register will give the name of the owner but not the demise charterer (if one exists).

Alternatively, the contract may have a definitions clause identifying the carrier as "the party on whose behalf this Bill of Lading has been signed" and upon referring to the signature box at the foot of the face of the bill it may transpire that the bill is signed by "XYZ as agent only" or "XYZ as agent for the carrier" but without saying as agent for whom or who is the carrier. Accurate identification of the carrier is a problem which has long worried documentary credit bankers and large numbers of carriers fail to identify themselves accurately and contractually in their bills.

Provisions in the 1993 Uniform Customs and Practice for Documentary Credits (UCP 500) which took effect on 1 January 1994 require the party on whose behalf the bill is signed to be identified in the signature box. This is designed to solve this problem for bankers and may cause some problems to carriers seeking to hide behind identity of carrier clauses on the reverse because, by the rules of precedence, in the event of conflict anything on the face of the Bill will override anything in the text overleaf.

(b) "Contract of carriage"

"(*b*) 'Contract of carriage' applies only to contracts of carriage covered by a bill of lading or any similar document of title, in so far as such document relates to the carriage of goods by sea, including any bill of lading or any similar document as aforesaid issued under or pursuant to a charter party from the moment at which such a bill of lading or similar document of title regulates the relations between a carrier and a holder of the same."

This definition needs to be taken in two parts:

   (i) not issued under or pursuant to a charterparty; and
   (ii) issued under or pursuant to a charterparty.

(i) Clearly the words "contract of carriage" cover bills of lading but what of "similar document of title"? A waybill is not a document of title, so cannot be considered to come within that definition. Does that mean that waybills are not mandatorily subject to the Rules? This will be discussed later when considering Article VI (*see* page 52).

There being no other documents of title in common usage in shipping, one must assume that the words "similar document of title" were added as an all-embracing "catch-all" in case the drafters forgot anything, or something subsequently developed. For instance, it has never been conclusively established that a combined transport bill of lading is a bill of lading within the meaning of the Act, although it must be now by custom and usage, if through no other qualification. Alternatively, with the trend towards computerisation, banks are investigating "paperless documentary credits" and it may happen one day that "computer shall speak [sense] unto computer"; that is the carrier's computer will send a message to the bank's computer to complete the documentary credit process and no paper bill will be issued. All things may be possible and it is just possible that these few words may one day mean the difference between the Act being adequate in its present form and the need for an amending Act.

(ii) Where a bill is issued under or pursuant to a charterparty then, as between owner and charterer, it is only a receipt and the charterparty is the contract of carriage and, as the Act does not cover charterparties, it is not subject to the Act. If the charterer negotiates that bill to an innocent third party purchaser for value, who is not a party to the charterparty contract, then the bill becomes the contract of carriage and the act becomes effective. The terms of the charterparty may still be incorporated into the contract of carriage by a suitable incorporation clause in the bill, but now these terms will only be valid to the extent that they do not conflict with the Rules. To the extent that they do so they shall be null and void.

In both cases note that the Act applies only during carriage of goods by sea and not during any pre- or post-carriage or handling.

(c) "Goods"

> "(c) 'Goods' includes goods, wares, merchandise, and articles of every kind whatsoever except live animals and cargo which by the contract of carriage is stated as being carried on deck and is so carried."

"Goods" is a fairly self-explanatory definition within the scope of the Rules, although due note must be taken of Article VI, the terms of which provide that the carrier may contract upon terms contrary to the Act for goods that are not "ordinary commercial shipments" provided no bill of lading has been issued (*see* page 52). *See* also earlier remarks relating to COGSA 1924, sections 1 and 4 (page 2) and COGSA 1971, section 1(7) (page 11), all of which qualify in some way the definition of "Goods" for the purpose of determining the applicability of the relevant Act. In this context COGSA 1971, section 1(7), is the one of which the carrier needs to beware most if he wishes to avoid unintended liability for live animals and deck cargo.

A small point to note is that the Rules talk of "live animals" whereas many bills of lading, particularly the older port-to-port variety, talk of "livestock". "Live animals" is clearly all-embracing but "livestock" carries a suggestion of domesticated animals—stock being a farming term. Carriers would be well advised to use the words "live animals" in their bills to mirror the language of the Act and give themselves protection if they carry wild animals.

Whether the term "live animals" covers live birds, insects, fish and/or reptiles is something which appears not to have been determined and, with the frequency with which they are carried being not particularly high, may remain so for some time. The doctrine of *contra proferentum* may well mean that the carrier, who would doubtless be the party trying to show that he is within the definition, would have the definition construed narrowly and against his interest, thereby putting him outside of the definition. The same goes for live plants, which are carried increasingly, particularly in containerised trades under temperature controlled conditions. Thus such things would probably come within the definition "goods", and the Rules would apply to their carriage, unless the carrier avoided the issue of a "bill of lading or similar document of title".

(d) "Ship"

"(*d*) 'Ship' means any vessel used for the carriage of goods by sea."

"Ship" is defined very simply as "any vessel used for the carriage of goods by sea" but still warrants careful study. "Any vessel"—so barge or ship, self-propelled or towed, sail, steam or motor, even a raft qualifies. "By sea"—so not applicable to estuarial, river or canal navigation (unless contractually applied, as is the case in many combined transport bills of lading).

(e) "Carriage of goods"

"(*e*) 'Carriage of goods' covers the period from the time when the goods are loaded on to the time they are discharged from the ship."

"Carriage of goods" also appears to be a clear definition but embodies a lack of precision in its wording which is a potential source of trouble. When are "the goods loaded" and when are they "discharged from the ship"? When does loading commence and discharge finish and, thus, when does the Act take effect and terminate? This is a point not made clear in the Act, so one has to look elsewhere for the answer.

To suggest, as some have done, that loading starts and finishes at the ship's rail is to attempt a totally impractical solution, which is clearly untenable given even a modicum of common sense. The thought that a carrier receives and delivers goods in mid-air at the end of a crane's hook is too ridiculous for words. How can condition be ascertained at that precise point? Whose servant/agent/sub-contractor is the stevedore who would surely refuse to be paid by the cargo interest from quay to ship's rail and thereafter by the carrier? It fell to Lord Devlin (Mr Justice Devlin as he then was) to provide the common sense answer to this by means of case law in the case of *Pyrene Co.* v. *Scindia*

Steam Navigation Co. [1954] 1 Lloyd's Rep. 321 to the effect that the Rules extend to cover the entire loading and discharging processes.

As the loading and discharging are essentially part of the contract of carriage in liner shipping and as "liner terms" means that the carrier pays for loading and discharging, this is clearly the logical answer in liner shipping. The Rules apply from receipt by the sea carrier until he delivers at destination. But "receipt" and "delivery" take place at different places in different ports so the "custom of the port" needs to be considered in deciding just where receipt/ delivery is effected and, thus, the scope of the Rules in any given contract of carriage.

ARTICLE II: RISKS

"Subject to the provisions of Article VI, under every contract of carriage of goods by sea the carrier, in relation to the loading, handling, stowage, carriage, custody, care and discharge of such goods, shall be subject to the responsibilities and liabilities, and entitled to the rights and immunities hereinafter set forth."

This article is a simple statement that the Rules shall apply once a "contract of carriage" is entered into and that they shall govern the carrier's responsibilities, liabilities, rights and immunities during the carriage of goods by sea, subject to the provisions of Article VI (*see* page 52). All the duties of the carrier during the carriage are covered and listed in this article: loading, handling, stowage, carriage, custody, care and discharge.

ARTICLE III: RESPONSIBILITIES AND LIABILITIES

Rule 1

"The carrier shall be bound before and at the beginning of the voyage to exercise due diligence to:
  (*a*) Make the ship seaworthy.
  (*b*) Properly man, equip and supply the ship.
  (*c*) Make the holds, refrigerating and cool chambers, and all other parts of the ship in which goods are carried, fit and safe for their reception, carriage and preservation."

This short Rule is perhaps one of the most important Rules in the entire Schedule and its interpretation has received the closest scrutiny by the legal profession.

The crux of the whole Rule hinges on the interpretation of "due diligence". Just what is "due diligence", when must it be exercised and by whom? There is a plethora of case law on this Rule and a knowledge of some of the leading cases is essential to understand the interpretation of it.

Maxine Footwear Co. Ltd. v. Canadian Government Merchant Marine Ltd.
[1959] 2 Lloyd's Rep. 105

In this Privy Council case it was established that "before and at the beginning
of the voyage" means before loading of cargo has commenced and until the
vessel weighs anchor or slips her lines to sail.

This case also confirmed an earlier Canadian decision to the effect that
compliance with the requirements of Article III, Rule 1, is an overriding
obligation placed upon the carrier before he can take advantage of any of the
exceptions granted in Article IV, Rule 2.

Grain Growers Export Co. v. Canada Steamship Lines Ltd. (1918) 43 O.L.R.
330

In this case "due diligence" was defined as "not merely a praiseworthy or
sincere, though unsuccessful, effort, but such an intelligent and efficient
attempt as shall make it so [seaworthy] as far as diligence can serve". To just
say "I did my best" is not enough. Thus, it can be seen that the release from
an absolute warranty of seaworthiness in the Act is not the great release that
it may appear, as the actions of the carrier in exercising due diligence are
judged against the highest standard. This standard will change as the fund of
knowledge and experience changes. For instance, the failure of an unexpected
component which could not be reasonably expected to fail might escape under
the "due diligence" doctrine the first time, but thereafter, on that or other
sister ships of the same owner (or others if knowledge is promulgated) the
standard of care will be increased to expect regular inspection of that component to prevent recurrence, or even redesign to overcome the problem. Thus,
in practice, the carrier is hard pushed to prove compliance with Article III,
Rule 1, in order to qualify for the benefits of Article IV, Rule 2.

Accordingly, "due diligence" may be defined as genuine, competent and
reasonable effort of the carrier to fulfil the prerequisites set out in Article III,
Rule 1.

Of course, what constitutes "due diligence" in a myriad of circumstances
will always require consideration of the facts of the case and there are numer-
ous examples of case law giving guidance on this point, although many have
since been overtaken by changes in the level of knowledge, technology,
method of operating (e.g. containerisation) and other factors. They are but a
snapshot at that time and, whilst aiding subsequent thinking, are not necessarily binding where the facts have changed.

Riverstone Meat Co. Pty. Ltd. v. Lancashire Shipping Co. (The Muncaster
Castle) [1961] 1 Lloyd's Rep. 57

This is, perhaps, the most famous of the "due diligence" cases. It decided that
the duty of "due diligence" was non-delegable and that the carrier had a
vicarious liability for the default of any servant, agent or sub-contractor in
exercising due diligence to make the ship seaworthy. Thus, the carrier could

not say that, by engaging a reputable sub-contractor, he had exercised due diligence and was thus entitled to the benefits of Article IV, Rule 2, if that sub-contractor failed to exercise due diligence.

Thus, through case law, we now have precise definitions of the meaning of "before and at the beginning of the voyage" "due diligence" and the fact that this duty is non-delegable without having vicarious liability for the actions of the delegate. From the preamble let us pass on to consider the sub-rules.

(a) Make the ship seaworthy

What does seaworthiness mean? A vessel may be said to be seaworthy when it is in such a condition with such efficient equipment, and manned by such a master and crew, that in normal circumstances cargo may be loaded, carried, cared for and discharged properly and safely on the contemplated voyage.

Thus it may be seen that seaworthiness covers many things, a staunch hull and hatches, an efficient and adequate system of pumps, valves, boilers, engines, generators and (where appropriate) refrigeration machinery, all in good working order. The vessel must be equipped with up-to-date charts, notices to mariners and adequate reliable navigational equipment (radar etc.). The master, officers and crew must be adequate in number and qualification and properly trained and instructed in the operation of the vessel and all its idiosyncrasies. Adequate instruction manuals and other instructions must be available and equipment must be properly labelled. Diagrams to aid operation must be available and posted in suitably prominent places and, all in all, nothing must be left to chance by the carrier in an effort to anticipate and guard against all reasonably foreseeable eventualities.

(b) Properly man, equip and supply the ship

All of these factors are part of seaworthiness and, presumably, are added lest anyone should attempt to give seaworthiness its narrow interpretation of only relating to the construction and condition of the hull and machinery of the vessel.

(c) Make the holds, refrigerating and cool chambers, and all other parts of the ship in which goods are carried, fit and safe for their reception, carriage and preservation

In short to make the ship cargoworthy. Cargoworthiness is an aspect of sea-worthiness. A cargoworthy vessel may still be unseaworthy, in that the cargo can be stored safely in the hold even though it cannot travel to its destination because of a defect in the ship's engines, crew, charts etc., but an uncargo-worthy vessel will always be unseaworthy.

What is required to comply with the requirements of this clause will clearly vary according to the cargo to be carried, the nature and length of the voyage and the characteristics of the vessel. It will include the thorough cleaning of tanks and refrigerated spaces that are to be used for the carriage of foodstuffs and other easily contaminated cargoes, the correct placing of cargo battens, dunnaging, kraft paper, separation and other cargo protections to prevent the cargo from touching the sides of the hull and being damaged by condensation which settles out on the steelwork of the hull (being the coldest point in the hold) and to protect against damage by other cargoes or any other source of damage to cargo.

Rule 2

"Subject to the provisions of Article IV, the carrier shall properly and carefully load, handle, stow, carry, keep, care for, and discharge the goods carried."

The important point to notice here is the absence of the qualification "exercise due diligence to", which is so prominent in Rule 1 of this Article, and its replacement by the requirement to carry out the tasks listed in this Rule "properly and carefully". Not properly OR carefully—properly AND carefully, fail on one and you fail altogether. In practice, given the high standard against which due diligence is judged, there is usually little difference, so that the difference is often more academic than real, although it is feasible that something could occur where this minor difference could be vital.

(Of course what is "properly and carefully" will vary infinitely according to the facts of each case, the nature of the cargo, the type of packing, the type of carriage (containerised/break-bulk) the type of ship, the type of voyage (short/deep-sea) the time of year, etc., etc., *ad nauseam.*)

Properly and carefully are strict terms allowing no latitude at all for failed effort and, furthermore, unlike Rule 1, there is no qualification "at the beginning of the voyage", so these obligations apply at all times throughout the voyage. However, these obligations are made "subject to Article IV" so that any of the defences outlined there are available in defence of a claim brought under this Rule. However, before he can plead an Article IV defence, a carrier must show that that was the proximate cause of loss, rather than any failure on his part to discharge his Article III, Rule 2, responsibilities. Where it appears that both causes have contributed to loss, the carrier has to show the extent of loss attributable to each cause, if he wishes to avoid responsibility for the loss caused by the Article IV excepted peril.

Rule 3

"After receiving the goods into his charge the carrier or the master or agent of the carrier shall, on demand of the shipper, issue to the shipper a bill of lading showing among other things:—
(*a*) The leading marks necessary for identification of the goods as the same are furnished in writing by the shipper before the loading of such goods starts, provided such marks are stamped or otherwise shown clearly upon the goods if uncovered, or on the cases or coverings in which such goods are contained, in such a manner as should ordinarily remain legible until the end of the voyage.

(b) Either the number of packages, or pieces, or the quantity, or weight, as the case may be, as furnished in writing by the shipper.

(c) The apparent order and condition of the goods.

Provided that no carrier, master or agent of the carrier shall be bound to state or show in the bill of lading any marks, number, quantity, or weight which he has reasonable ground for suspecting not accurately to represent the goods actually received, or which he has had no reasonable means of checking."

Like section 3 of COGSA 1924 this clause is somewhat of a "paper tiger" as it stipulates that a carrier will do something without providing any penalty for non-compliance, thereby opening the way to abuse. This is widely practised in the form mentioned when considering sections 1 and 4 of COGSA 1924 and section 1(3) of COGSA 1971 (*see* page 2), particularly in the ferry and short sea trades, where the absence of need for a bill of lading as a document of title, with which to negotiate a documentary credit transaction, means that many merchants do not take so much interest in the form of the contract of carriage and many do not realise how their rights are thereby eroded. The use of consignment notes and non-negotiable receipts is prevalent in ferry and short sea traffic and many operators, having achieved the important point of avoiding mandatory application of the Rules by not issuing a bill of lading, often then proceed to "dress up" their terms and conditions to appear reasonable to the casual observer by contractually incorporating the Rules, but with their terms and conditions retaining paramountcy. They then put a condition in to the effect that the container or lorry is a package and that the weight alternative is deleted in the Hague-Visby Rules. This means that maximum recourse becomes £100 per container or lorry under Hague Rules and 666·67 SDRs per container or lorry under the Hague-Visby Rules. Hardly an adequate level of liability.

However, assuming that a bill of lading is to be issued, the following points should be noted in relation to this Rule.

The preamble provides for the carrier to "issue" a bill of lading. Traditionally this was accomplished by the merchant preparing the bill from the information on the mate's receipt and then obtaining the carrier's signature thereto. Thus "issue" was accomplished by mere signature. Today, in containerised combined transport, it is quite common for carriers to produce bills of lading by computer from details put into the computer for manifest purposes, so "issue" takes on its normal grammatical meaning.

Sub-rule (a) lists the descriptive detail which the shipper may expect the carrier to show on the bill. Only leading marks are necessary and superfluous detail should be avoided. It is not, as many believe, necessary for documentary credit purposes, indeed Article 37(c) of the present Uniform Customs and Practice for Documentary Credits (ICC Brochure 500—operative since 1 January 1994) provides:

"The description of the goods in the commercial invoice must correspond with the description in the credit. In all other documents, the goods may be described in general terms not inconsistent with the description of the goods in the credit."

and for these purposes a bill of lading qualifies as an "other document", so "general terms" only are necessary.

Note that the shipper has to supply details of the leading marks "in writing . . . before the loading of such goods starts" (sub-rule (a)) and the tally of the goods "in writing" (sub-rule (b)) and that the marks have to be "shown clearly", upon the goods or their packaging "in such a manner as should ordinarily remain legible until the end of the voyage". The requirement regarding legibility will vary according to the individual circumstances. Regarding the size of marks which "show clearly", some operators lay down minimum sizes of letters/figures in their conditions in an effort to assist themselves in claiming the defence of insufficiency of marks (see Art. IV, Rule 2(o) page 12) where the burden would be on them to show that this, rather than some other reason, was the proximate cause (proximate in efficiency rather than time) of loss or damage.

Sub-rule (b) provides the requirement for an acknowledgement of weight or tally, but note that this is weight or tally as provided by the shipper who, under Rule 5 of this Article, warrants the accuracy thereof to the carrier.

Sub rule (c), however, carries no such qualification and is a direct requirement of the carrier to issue a receipt evidencing the APPARENT order and condition of the goods, that is to say the condition of the goods as they appear to the carrier when presented to him for shipment already packed. He is not expected to open packages and check internal condition, only apparent external condition. Clearly a leaking package (or container) is evidence of bad order within, so that the apparent order and condition of the package is bad and requires investigation/comment by the carrier, who cannot just ignore it with impunity.

Sub-rules (a) and (b) are subject to a proviso to the effect that the carrier is not obliged to show any of the detail required in those sub-rules "which he has reasonable ground for suspecting not accurately to represent the goods actually received, or which he has no reasonable means of checking".

In COGSA 1924 this is modified somewhat by section 5 of the Act (see page 3) in relation to the carriage of bulk cargoes, but no such modification is made in COGSA 1971.

In containerised carriage this proviso applies particularly to shipper-packed containers, where all that the carrier can acknowledge is one container. However, more detail than this is necessary for commercial purposes, so the carrier provides this on a "said to contain" basis as "Details declared by Shipper but not acknowledged by the Carrier".

Rule 4

"Such a bill of lading shall be prima facie evidence of the receipt by the carrier of the goods as therein described in accordance with paragraph 3(a), (b) and (c)."

This is the first instance of any difference between the Hague Rules and the Hague-Visby Rules. Both carry the sentence set out above but, whereas that is the entire Rule in the Hague Rules, the additional sentence below is added in the Hague-Visby Rules.

"However, proof to the contrary shall not be admissible when the bill of lading has been transferred to a third party acting in good faith."

In practice, however, the change is one of clarification only, as the need to protect the first class status of a bill of lading as a document of title has always meant that the courts have applied the doctrine of estoppel evident in the Hague-Visby Rules to the Hague Rules anyway.

Whereas Rule 3(*a*) and (*b*) of Article III provide for the shipper to provide cargo detail, Rule 4 makes sure that the carrier checks it carefully by making that detail the basis of the carrier's responsibility for the goods covered by that bill of lading.

Rule 4 of the Hague Rules puts the onus of proof that goods were received in a condition other than as described in the bill of lading clearly on the carrier, but would appear to stop short of estoppel by making the evidence *prima facie* only. This again is more illusory than real and the additional sentence added in the Hague-Visby Rules goes little further than the Carriage of Goods by Sea Act 1992 which reads:

Representations in bills of lading

"**4.** A bill of lading which—
   (*a*) represents goods to have been shipped on board a vessel or to have been received for shipment on board a vessel; and
   (*b*) has been signed by the master of the vessel or by a person who was not the master but had the express, implied or apparent authority of the carrier to sign bills of lading.
shall, in favour of a person who has become the lawful holder of the bill, be conclusive evidence against the carrier of the shipment of the goods or, as the case may be, of their receipt for shipment."

Most other countries have similar enactments in their national legislation, so that the doctrine of estoppel applies once the bill has passed legitimately for value out of the hands of the shipper, this being a natural consequence of the need to protect the first class status of the bill as a document of title in order to promote international trade through the documentary credit process, where payment is made against a document upon which reliance can be placed to accurately represent the goods shipped, ownership of which is tantamount to ownership of the goods.

Rule 5

"The shipper shall be deemed to have guaranteed to the carrier the accuracy at the time of shipment of the marks, number, quantity and weight, as furnished by him, and the shipper shall indemnify the carrier against all loss, damages and expenses arising or resulting from inaccuracies in such particulars. The right of the carrier to such indemnity shall in no way limit his responsibility and liability under the contract of carriage to any person other than the shipper."

If Rule 4 seems somewhat harsh on the carrier, Rule 5 brings him a degree of relief in the form of an indemnity from the shipper from the consequences of inaccuracy in the details which he provides consequent to Rule 3. However, this is an indemnity and not a defence, so that it is a right against the shipper after loss, damage, expense or liability is incurred and cannot be used as a defence against a claim by a third party purchaser of the bill for value, or indeed anyone other than the shipper.

Rule 6

Whilst Rule 6 has been altered by the Visby Amendments, the first part remains unchanged and reads:

"Unless notice of loss or damage and the general nature of such loss or damage be given in writing to the carrier or his agent at the port of discharge before or at the time of the removal of the goods into the custody of the person entitled to delivery thereof under the contract of carriage, or, if the loss or damage be not apparent, within three days such removal shall be prima facie evidence of the delivery by the carrier of the goods as described in the bill of lading.

The notice in writing need not be given if the state of the goods has, at the time of their receipt, been the subject of joint survey or inspection."

thereafter the Hague Rules text reads:

"In any event the carrier and the ship shall be discharged from all liability in respect of loss or damage unless suit is brought within one year after delivery of the goods or the date when the goods should have been delivered.

In the case of any actual or apprehended loss or damage the carrier and the receiver shall give all reasonable facilities to each other for inspecting and tallying the goods."

whilst the Hague-Visby text reads:

"Subject to paragraph 6 *bis* the carrier and the ship shall in any event be discharged from all liability whatsoever in respect of the goods, unless suit is brought within one year of their delivery or of the date when they should have been delivered. This period may, however, be extended if the parties so agree after the case of action has arisen. In the case of any actual or apprehended loss or damage the carrier and the receiver shall give all reasonable facilities to each other for inspecting and tallying the goods.

6 *bis.* An action for indemnity against a third person may be brought even after the expiration of the year provided for in the preceding paragraph if brought within the time allowed by the law of the Court seized of the case. However, the time allowed shall be not less than three months, commencing from the day when the person bringing such an action for indemnity has settled the claim or has been served with process in the action against himself."

As can be seen this Rule covers two matters:
    (i)   Notice of claim; and
    (ii) Time bar;
and it is important to understand clearly the difference between the two and the effect of breach of the relevant provisions of this Rule relating to either.

(i) Notice of claim

This must be given in writing and must be given before or at the time of delivery (i.e. when the contract of carriage is terminated) where loss or damage is apparent, or within three days of delivery if loss or damage is not apparent at delivery. This apparently simple sentence contains at least three words/phrases in need of further clarification.

(a) *In writing*—This may be by clausing the receipt where loss or damage is apparent at the time of delivery and this is by far the commonest way in which a merchant complies with the requirements of this Rule. Indeed, where loss or damage is apparent at the time of delivery, it is the only way open to him under this Rule, as it is only where loss or damage is not apparent at the time of delivery that the merchant has three days within which to make his claim. In this case it may take any written form: letter, telex etc.

This requirement is, however, waived where a joint survey or inspection of the goods is made at the time of delivery.

(b) *Delivery*—The actual wording says "removal of the goods into the custody of the person entitled to delivery thereof under the contract of carriage". Local custom of the port will dictate precisely when this occurs, applying criteria along the lines outlined in considering Article I(*e*) (*see* page 18) in determining precisely when this takes place.

(c) *Three days*—An unfortunately imprecise limit which does not appear to have been clarified by case law. Three calendar days or working days? Without qualification it would appear to mean three consecutive calendar days, but what if the third day falls on a holiday when notice cannot be given? Case law on time limitation (*Pristam* v. *S. Russell & Sons Ltd.* [1973] Q.B. 366) suggests that, in such a case, notice given on the next working day is timely.

In any event, it is unlikely that this point will ever loom sufficiently important in a case for it to be resolved, unless it be in *obiter dictum* from a judge addressing himself to the point en route to deciding some more important issue. This is because the importance of limitation of time within which to give notice of claim is usually overstated. The penalty for failure is that the merchant must show that the loss/damage, which forms the subject of his claim, was in existence at the time of delivery and has not either been caused or aggravated since. It does not, as some suggest, create a situation where an onus devolves upon the merchant to prove negligence on the part of the carrier.

Onus is another emotive word on which many put the criminal law interpretation: that the guilt of the defendant must be proved beyond all reasonable doubt. In civil law it is not a case of guilt but of a plaintiff succeeding or failing in an action against a defendant in contract or in tort and, in such a case, the decision depends upon the judge's interpretation of facts and law and who presents the most credible case. Onus does not come into it as strongly as many think in a commercial court as it is rather a case of on which side the weight of evidence comes down in the eyes of the presiding judge.

The provisions of Rule 6 relating to notice of claim are identical in both the Hague and the Hague-Visby Rules.

(ii)   Time bar

The difference in the treatment of time bars between the Hague Rules and the Hague-Visby Rules arises primarily in Rule 6 *bis,* to which reference will be made later, but there is an additional clarifying sentence in the Hague-Visby Rules making it quite clear that extensions of time within which to bring suit, which may be agreed between the parties, are valid. There was a school of thought that suggested that such extensions were invalid by being contrary to the mandatory law of COGSA 1924, which provides unequivocally that claims are time-barred unless suit is brought within one year of delivery but Article V would seem to allow such arrangements. Otherwise the provisions of the Hague Rules and the Hague-Visby Rules on time bars are virtually identical, giving the claimant one year from the date of delivery (or the date when the goods should have been delivered to cover losses of total consignments) within which to bring suit, if a claim is not settled beforehand, in order to avoid his claim becoming time-barred. Note that the only requirement is to bring suit. This means to take out a writ; it does not require it to be served. As the English court allows four months for the service of writs, it could be up to 16 months before a carrier can be certain that there will be no valid enforceable claim, in respect of cargo delivered, of which he is unaware.

One small difference between the Hague and Hague-Visby Rules in the time bar provision is the addition in the latter of the word "whatsoever" after "liability" in the first sentence of this section. The addition of this single word may have quite an important effect. It ensures that the time bar continues to operate even in the event of breach of Article IV Rule 5(*e*) (*see* page 48) preventing the carrier from benefiting from limitation of liability. Whether this interpretation would apply to the Hague Rules which merely refers to "all liability" is problematical.

Rule 6 *bis* of the Hague-Visby Rules was added to overcome the problem experienced by carriers who sub-contract all or part of the carriage and remain primarily liable to the merchant for the performance of the contract by reason of the absence of any demise clause in their Bill of Lading. If a claim is made or suit is commenced against such a carrier at the last minute, this leaves him with little or no time within which to protect his right of recourse to his sub-contracting carrier. This addition overcomes that problem by giving the first carrier three months from the date when he either:

(a)   settles the claim (by amicable negotiation); or
(b)   is served with a writ in respect of that claim;

within which to bring his claim against his sub-contractor. (This is because "the law of the Court seized of the case" usually applies the Hague-Visby Rules one-year time limit and Rule 6 *bis* gives "*not less* than three months . . .". It is expressed in this way in case the Hague-Visby Rules are not contractually applied to the sub-contractor, and the matter of time limitation is not covered in the contract of carriage, in which case the six years of the Statute of Limitations would apply. It is not the object of the Rules to reduce time limits, only to provide for minimum periods.)

Both the Hague Rules and the Hague-Visby Rules incorporate a requirement for both carrier and receiver to give each other "all reasonable facilities . . . for inspecting and tallying the goods" where there is any actual or suspected loss or damage to the goods. Note that this requirement for reasonable facilities covers inspection and tallying of the goods only and does not extend to require the carrier to give inspection facilities to the receiver in respect of the vessel.

Rule 7

"After the goods are loaded the bill of lading to be issued by the carrier, master, or agent of the carrier, to the shipper shall, if the shipper so demands, be a 'shipped' bill of lading, provided that if the shipper shall have previously taken up any document of title to such goods, he shall surrender the same as against the issue of the 'shipped' bill of lading, but at the option of the carrier such document of title may be noted at the port of shipment by the carrier, master, or agent with the name or names of the ship or ships upon which the goods have been shipped and the date or dates of shipment, and when so noted, if it shows the particulars mentioned in paragraph 3 of Article III, shall for the purpose of this article be deemed to constitute a 'shipped' bill of lading."

A bill of lading may be either a "Received for Shipment" or a "Shipped" document. Traditionally the requirement has been almost exclusively for shipped bills, as these evidence that the transit has commenced and the goods are not just sitting on the quay (usually at shipper's risk) awaiting the arrival of the ship. Thus, the overriding majority of letters of credit require shipped bills to protect the buyer's interest. The seller would usually prefer RFS (Received for Shipment) bills, as these can be issued earlier than shipped bills (which must await confirmation of loading on board) so that he can negotiate his documentary credit earlier and secure a more prompt payment.

With the advent of Combined Transport Bills of Lading (CTBsL) the need for shipped bills ought to diminish, but old practices die hard. With most CTBsL the carrier accepts responsibility and liability for the goods on a door-to-door basis, so that evidence of shipment is not so vital in combined transport. Accordingly, the RFS-CTBsL ought to be acceptable, but rarely is, as the buyer is still looking for evidence of loading on the vessel, this being, in his view, the most important proof that the goods have commenced the major part of their transit to him.

The method of bill of lading production also tends to vary. The traditional method, usually found in conventional port to port shipping, is for the shipper to present his cargo at the ship's side and receive a "mate's receipt" evidencing tally and condition. From this he would prepare his set of bills of lading on the bill of lading stationery of the carrying line to reflect the terms of the "mate's receipt". He would then take his bills to the office of the carrier (or his agent) for signature.

This approach still applies in some areas today but, particularly with combined transport, the bills of lading are frequently produced by the carrier's computer from detail input from the shipper's instructions and receipt issued on receipt of the cargo in order to provide a manifest tape of the ship's cargo. These are then posted to the shipper, thus obviating the need for him to prepare documents and then present them to the carrier for authentication.

Rule 7 provides that a shipper is entitled to a shipped bill once the goods are loaded, if he wants one, but must surrender any other document of title in exchange therefor (i.e. an RFS bill). In practice an RFS bill is converted into a shipped bill by means of a "Shipped on Board" (SOB) stamp on the face of the bill, which is duly dated and signed, and the Rule gives the carrier the option of this method. (In liner shipping masters rarely sign bills, leaving this to the carrier (at his home port) or his agents.)

The Rule provides that a shipped bill is one which bears the detail required in Article III, Rule 3, together with:

(a)   the name or names of the ship or ships upon which the goods have been shipped (split shipments, which are so often disallowed in letters of credit, are not barred by the Rules);
(b)   the date or dates of shipment.

Thus, whilst it would be unusual to find one, there is no restriction in law to having one bill of lading evidencing shipment of cargo on more than one vessel.

A question often asked by many carrier's clerks is: "what detail may I safely show on a bill of lading?" The simple answer to this is: "anything, so long as it is true and capable of performance without being unduly restrictive upon you."

An example of a clause incapable of performance or unduly restrictive would be a request for a clause stating: "To be carried at −15°C." This is impossible. "To be carried at below −15°C" is possible, or "To be carried at between −15°C and −20°C" is also possible, but −15°C without variation during the voyage to −14·9°C or −15·1°C is not.

Rule 8

"Any clause, covenant, or agreement in a contract of carriage relieving the carrier or the ship from liability for loss or damage to, or in connection with, goods arising from negligence, fault, or failure in the duties and obligations provided in this article or lessening such liability otherwise than as provided in these Rules, shall be null and void and of no effect. A benefit of insurance in favour of the carrier or similar clause shall be deemed to be a clause relieving the carrier from liability."

In considering this Rule, one should be aware of the provisions of Articles V and VI. Article V allows the carrier to contract terms more onerous to himself than those provided in the Rules, whilst Article VI allows him to contract on less onerous terms for certain classes of goods, PROVIDED that he does not issue a bill of lading or other negotiable instrument. If he issues a bill of lading, he will automatically become subject to the Rules and all the requirements placed upon him by the Rules.

Rule 8 makes it quite clear that, once he has issued a bill of lading, he cannot protect himself against any of the provisions of the Article III exclusion clauses and the like. This Rule particularly makes clear that a bill of lading clause attempting to make the benefit of the shipper's cargo insurance inure to the carrier is invalid as a clause attempting to relieve the carrier from liability placed upon him by the Rules. In any event, most cargo insurance clauses contain a "not to inure" clause, in which the insurer specifically provides that, whilst the insurance is transferable to buyers, it cannot be used as protection by a carrier.

The effect of Rule 8 is to give the Rules paramount effect over any bill of lading clauses in the event of conflict.

ARTICLE IV: RIGHTS AND IMMUNITIES

Rule 1

"Neither the carrier nor the ship shall be liable for loss or damage arising or resulting from unseaworthiness unless caused by want of due diligence on the part of the carrier to make the ship seaworthy, and to secure that the ship is properly manned, equipped and supplied, and to make the holds, refrigerating and cool chambers and all other parts of the ship in which goods are carried fit and safe for their reception, carriage and preservation in accordance with the provisions of paragraph 1 of Article III. Whenever loss or damage has resulted from unseaworthiness the burden of proving the exercise of due diligence shall be on the carrier or other person claiming exemption under this article."

Rule 1 merely serves to introduce Article IV by reminding of the obligations laid upon the carrier in Article III, Rule 1, which he must discharge before he can claim the benefits of Article IV. The Rule starts by making the point that seaworthiness is not a strict or absolute warranty on the carrier, who needs only to prove due diligence to provide a seaworthy vessel before and at the commencement of the voyage, a point emphasised in section 2 of COGSA 1924 and section 3 of COGSA 1971. It goes on to paraphrase and cross-reference to Article III, Rule 1 (*see* page 19), and concludes by a statement putting the onus of proving a defence upon the party seeking to use that defence, which in most cases is, of course, the carrier.

Rule 2

"Neither the carrier nor the ship shall be responsible for loss or damage arising or resulting from:—

   (a) Act, neglect, or default of the master, mariner, pilot, or the servants of the carrier in the navigation or in the management of the ship.

   (b) Fire, unless caused by the actual fault or privity of the carrier.

   (c) Perils, dangers and accidents of the sea or other navigable waters.

   (d) Act of God.

   (e) Act of war.

   (f) Act of public enemies.

   (g) Arrest or restraint of princes, rulers or people, or seizure under legal process.

   (h) Quarantine restrictions.

   (i) Act or omission of the shipper or owner of the goods, his agent or representative.

   (j) Strikes or lockouts or stoppage or restraint of labour from whatever cause, whether partial or general.

   (k) Riots and civil commotions.

   (l) Saving or attempting to save life or property at sea.

   (m) Wastage in bulk of weight or any other loss or damage arising from inherent defect, quality or vice of the goods.

   (n) Insufficiency of packing.

   (o) Insufficiency or inadequacy of marks.

   (p) Latent defects not discoverable by due diligence.

   (q) Any other cause arising without the actual fault or privity of the carrier, or without the fault or neglect of the agents or servants of the carrier, but the burden of proof shall be on the person claiming the benefit of this exception to show that neither the actual fault or privity of the carrier nor the fault or neglect of the agents or servants of the carrier contributed to the loss or damage."

If Article III, Rule 1, is the most important Rule, it is only so by a short margin over this Rule 2 of Article IV. Between the two of them they are at the bottom of the vast majority of cases involving the Hague Rules and the Hague-Visby Rules, and, of the two, Rule 2 of Article IV is probably the better known.

    The list of exclusions appears daunting and exhaustive until one remembers that compliance with Article III, Rule 1, is a prerequisite to claiming defence under these immunities and, as has been noted when discussing that Rule, this is a somewhat onerous task, which only the most diligent carriers can hope to achieve. Furthermore, as it is invariably the carrier seeking to apply the Rule as a defence to a cargo claim, its application is subject to the *contra proferentum* rule, under which its seemingly limitless exclusions are interpreted as narrowly as possible against the interest of the party seeking to apply it so, effectively, the onus of proof is upon the carrier to bring himself within the defence. In order to do this the carrier must prove:

    (a) the cause of loss or damage;

    (b) that due diligence has been exercised to make the vessel seaworthy; and then

(c) that the cause of loss comes within one of the Article IV, Rule 2, exclusions.

However, if the loss or damage can be shown to have arisen or resulted from one of the sub-rules to Article IV, Rule 2, and provided that the carrier has complied with Article III, Rules 1 and 2, the carrier may disclaim responsibility for such loss or damage.

Detailed examination of the individual sub-rules of this Rule explains this situation more clearly.

(a) Act, neglect, or default of the master, mariner, pilot, or the servants of the carrier in the navigation or in the management of the ship

The most important point to notice in this sub-rule is that the exclusion operates only in respect of error "in the navigation or in the management of the ship". Act, neglect or default in the care of the cargo does not come within this exclusion. This means that the error has to be one primarily affecting the ship. A simple definition might be that it is an erroneous act or omission, the original purpose of which was primarily directed towards the ship, her safety and well being and towards the venture generally (i.e. both ship and cargo).

Whilst Article IV, Rule 2(*a*), makes no mention of error in the care of the cargo, this requirement is made in Article III, Rule 2, and, as there is nothing in Article IV to contradict it, it remains something for which the carrier is responsible and a prerequisite to claiming defence under Article IV, Rule 2.

There are many grey areas where it is unclear whether an error or omission is in relation to something directed towards the ship, her safety and well being and towards the venture generally, or in relation to care of the cargo (i.e. a breach of Article III, Rule 2). If both ship and cargo are affected by the same error, the carrier can usually avoid responsibility, as the whole venture is involved, but each case will be decided on the individual facts of the case. Where two errors occur, one being management of ship and the other care of cargo, the carrier must distinguish between the damage caused by each or be responsible for it all.

Finally, note that the error has to be on the part of "the master, mariner, pilot or the servants of the carrier". If the error is on the part of the owner himself, not only will the protection of the Rules be denied to the carrier, but he may also find himself precluded from enjoying the MSA limitation based on the tonnage of the vessel (relevant if the claim is a large one) where the 1957 Limitation Convention is operative, but not where the 1976 Convention on Limitation of Liability for Maritime Claims applies (*see* comment on COGSA 1924, section 6(2), page 4).

If the master is owner or part-owner of the ship and the 1957 Limitation Convention applies, the Rules will protect him in respect of negligence in any of his duties as master, but not as owner and another substantial grey area is created in determining whether any particular duty is that of a master or owner, where these two duties are vested in one and the same person.

(b) Fire, unless caused by the actual fault or privity of the carrier

Ironically, fire is one of the greatest hazards at sea, a point not readily appreciated by laymen who think that, surrounded by all that water with which to put it out, fire hazards must be minimal. Nevertheless, fire has been a major hazard at sea since time immemorial, long before mechanical power was invented. Spontaneous combustion in cargo, galley fires and many other causes have all been responsible for horrifying losses at sea, hence the special exclusion of fire which is not usually given to other carriers by land or baillees of cargo ashore. However, in granting the carrier the exception of fire in the Rules, the drafters were only perpetuating a defence already granted to carriers by section 502 of the Merchant Shipping Act of 1894.

Fire means flame, not just heat or smoke, another example of how the defence is narrowly interpreted against the person claiming the benefit of it.

Water damage to cargo, occasioned in the course of extinguishing a fire, is, of course, general average damage, that is to say damage caused as the result of a deliberate act attempting to save the adventure, as opposed to accidental damage. However, the carrier must guard against indiscriminate use of water in dousing a fire, as this could be construed as failure to care for the cargo, for which the carrier is liable.

The exclusion of fire is subject to the carrier (that is the owner of the vessel or his alter ego but not the master or crew) not being guilty of actual fault or privity in respect of the causation of the fire.

(c) Perils, dangers and accidents of the sea or other navigable waters

On the face of it perils of the sea appears to be an all-embracing exclusion, but the perils, dangers or accidents have to be extraordinary in nature. Damage caused by a force 8 gale with unremarkable seas encountered in the Bay of Biscay in January is unlikely to be held to be perils of the sea, because in that place at that time a ship should be prepared for foul weather. Thus, what constitutes "perils of the sea" is a matter of fact, in the light of what a reasonable mariner ought reasonably to expect and be prepared for at that place, at that time of year.

Not only is there no recognised standard by which one may gauge "perils of the sea", the standard varying with seasons and the type of conditions usually encountered in that place at that time, but the courts of different countries take substantially differing views. As with limitation, it is the US courts that take the most stringent view, so that to succeed with this defence in a US court is somewhat of a rarity, whereas English and Australian courts tend towards a more balanced view.

A recent Australian case of note is that of *The Bunga Seroja* (*Great China Metal Industries Co. Ltd v. MISC* (1995) 39 N.S.W.L.R. 683), decided in the Court of Appeal of the Supreme Court of New South Wales before Mr Justice Carruthers. In this case it was held that, the mere fact that damage was occasioned by a storm which was expectable did not of itself exclude a finding that the damage was occasioned by perils of the sea. (Leave has been granted to appeal to the High Court which is not likely before 1998.) However, it is difficult to see this appeal succeeding, as the judgment in this case appears to follow *obiter dictum* in a previous High Court judgment in the case of *The Visha Vibhut* (*Shipping Corp'n of India Ltd. v. Gamlen Chemical Co. (A/Asia) Pty Ltd.* H.C.A. 1980 P. 142), in which Mason and Wilson observed that it was unnecessary for the losses or the cause of the losses to be "extraordinary" for a defence of perils of the sea to succeed and that "sea and weather conditions which may reasonably be foreseen and guarded against may constitute a peril of the sea".

Oddly enough, some of the best potted definitions of "perils of the sea" come from American judges. Judge Hough in *The Rosalia* defined it as meaning "something so catastrophic as to triumph over those safeguards by which skilful and vigilant seamen usually bring ship and cargo to port in safety", whilst Judge Learned Hand in *The Naples Maru* observed that Judge Hough's definition "meant nothing more than that the weather encountered must be too much for a well-found vessel to withstand". A definition put together from several English cases is "any damage to goods carried, caused by seawater, storms, collision, stranding, or other perils peculiar to the sea or to a ship at sea, which could not be foreseen and guarded against by the shipowner or his servants as necessary or probable incidents of the adventure".

At times when "perils of the sea" threaten, many of the factors which go towards constituting a seaworthy vessel are put to the test. Thus, to succeed with this exclusion, the carrier must first prove compliance with Article III, Rules 1 and 2, and, whilst the test is what due diligence before and at the time of sailing would have revealed, the carrier has the disadvantage that the plaintiff and the court start with the benefit of hindsight, after his efforts have been put to the test.

A leading case which demonstrates this is *Blackwood Hodge v. Ellerman Lines* [1963] 1 Lloyd's Rep. 454, where the vessel encountered a hurricane, but loss was attributed to an inadequacy in the stow, so that the vessel was unseaworthy and Article III, Rules 1 and 2, were breached.

Another point to bear in mind is that seaworthiness is relative to the intended voyage. A ship that is seaworthy (i.e. adequately prepared) to cross the English Channel on a summer's day may well be unseaworthy for an Atlantic crossing in mid-winter.

From the above it can be appreciated that, whilst it does not necessarily follow that there must be serious damage to the ship for a plea of "perils of the sea" to succeed, few cases citing this defence have succeeded without it. Thus, whilst this is one of the most frequently claimed exclusions, it is a notoriously difficult one to prove, requiring satisfaction of the Article III, Rules 1 and 2, requirements after they have been put to the test, usually by extraordinary conditions and not just a bad storm.

(d) Act of God

The "Act of God" exclusion includes any accident which the carrier can show arose exclusively from natural causes, *without any human intervention*, which could not have been averted by any reasonable amount of foresight or care on the part of the carrier (i.e. flood, lightning and unexpected low temperature damage). It is, to some extent, a duplication of Rule 2(*q*) and overlaps into 2(*c*) on occasions (tidal wave caused by earthquake, volcanic eruption etc.).

(e) Act of war

"Act of war" is relatively self explanatory and needs little explanation, a fact which probably explains why there is little case law on this exclusion. The act of war does not have to be committed by a nation with whom the country of the flag of registry of the ship is in a state of declared war (Queen's enemies as it is called in English War Risks Club cover) and loss or damaged sustained when "caught in the middle" between warring factions with whom no state of war exists (non-Queen's enemies) counts equally as an act of war for the purpose of this exclusion. European vessels hit by Iraqi or Iranian missiles whilst trading into the Arabian Gulf are a good example of non-Queen's enemy damage.

(f) Act of public enemies

The precise meaning of "Act of public enemies" is uncertain, but is generally assumed to cover piracy, which is defined as "robbery and depredation on the sea or navigable rivers etc. or by descent from the sea upon the coast, by persons not holding a commission from an established civilised state". It may also extend to cover robbery with violence where this occurs in circumstances where the carrier could not have prevented it by exercising reasonable skill and/or care. It is very much an exclusion where successful pleading will depend upon the individual facts of the case.

(g) Arrest or restraint of princes, rulers or people, or seizure under legal process

Probably the most likely examples of this exclusion which come to mind are the blocking of the Suez Canal and Shatt-al-Arab waterways causing vessels and their cargoes to be trapped. For the exclusion to apply, there must be forcible interference by a state or the government of a country in, either taking possession of goods, or preventing the owners enjoying their rights of ownership over them by restricting the movement of the goods (blockade or trapping). It might occur at the outbreak of a war, where to deliver goods as manifested would constitute trading with an enemy of the flag of the vessel. Thus, the exception can operate where the restraint is not directly upon the vessel, which is outside the jurisdiction of the restraining power, but upon the person of the carrier and through him on the vessel.

(h) Quarantine restrictions

In as much as quarantine is usually enforced by governmental agencies, this exclusion is very close to the preceding one.

(i) Act or omission of the shipper or owner of the goods, his agent or representative

This exclusion, in conjunction with exclusion 2(*o*), reinforces Article III, Rule 5 It is a fairly self-explanatory and obviously reasonable exclusion, protecting the carrier from the act or neglect of his customers becoming a basis of claim against him.

(j) Strikes or lockouts or stoppage or restraint of labour from whatever cause, whether partial or general

The strikes etc. exclusion is only available to a carrier provided that he acts reasonably, without negligence and is not guilty of misrepresentation. For example, damage caused to cargo by delay where a carrier deliberately enters a strikebound port, where there is no prospect of the strike breaking, is unreasonably caused and the carrier may be denied the benefit of this exclusion, depending on the circumstances. The carrier must also show that any damage to the cargo is caused by the delay occasioned by the strike and not any negligence on his part (failure to care for the cargo) such as failure to ventilate causing condensation. Furthermore, where a carrier commits a fundamental breach of contract, by misleading the merchant into thinking goods have been shipped which are, in fact, strikebound on the quay, by issuing a "shipped" bill for them, he will, most certainly be denied the benefit of this exclusion.

(k) Riots and civil commotions

Whereas loss or damage caused by the delay inherent in a strike is covered in Rule 2(*j*), damage caused by strikers picketing would probably come within this exclusion. It is generally accepted that, between Rule 2(*e*) (*f*) and (*k*), it is intended that the carrier shall not be liable for loss or damage caused by the violent acts of third parties over whom the carrier has no control.

(l) Saving or attempting to save life or property at sea

This sub-rule combines with Article IV, Rule 4 (*see* page 40) to give the carrier protection when answering distress calls, thus enabling him to respond to such emergencies giving his full attention to them, without having to stop and consider his position when doing so *vis-à-vis* the cargo. This exclusion covers loss or damage to cargo during such attempts whilst Rule 4 covers the deviation aspect.

Note that the exclusion covers efforts to save life *or property*. This is quite important, as it is frequently difficult to differentiate between acts designed to save life and those to save property during an emergency and any restriction might make the potential salvor hesitate, at a time when such hesitation could be fatal.

(m)   Wastage in bulk or weight or any other loss or damage arising from inherent defect, quality or vice of the goods

Inherent vice, in this context, means the unfitness of the goods to withstand the ordinary incidents of the voyage, given the degree of care which the carrier is required by the contract to exercise in relation to the goods.

To the extent that damage is due to the carrier's breach of contract, he may not rely on this exclusion. Furthermore, his degree of knowledge, or the degree of knowledge that he ought reasonably to have had based on past experience, may affect the degree to which he can claim this exclusion. A carrier, who has operated for any time in a trade where a frequent cargo is wet salted hides, could not plead this exclusion to a claim for heat damage to goods stowed near an engine room bulkhead.

(n)   Insufficiency of packing

With the exclusion of insufficiency of packing, unlike that of inherent vice, the carrier, in order to succeed, must overcome his acknowledgment in the bill of lading that the goods have been received/shipped in apparent good order and condition. This means that the insufficiency must not be obvious at the time of receipt/shipment. Some carriers clause bills drawing attention to insufficiency of packing (especially for cargoes in paper bags/sacks). This is a somewhat futile exercise, as it draws attention to the fact that the carrier is aware of the deficiency and, far from protecting him, actually charges him with a responsibility to take extra care.

One very good example of this exception (which was not litigated) was a shipment of reels of Cellophane designed for use on high-speed cigarette-packing machines. These were shipped in heavy wooden cases, but on unpacking at the factory were found squashed/bruised, so that they were useless for their intended purpose. The cases were received and delivered in apparent good order and condition and the absence of internal bracing to prevent the springing of the boards of the case was not visible to external inspection. A clear case of insufficiency of packing.

(o)   Insufficiency or inadequacy of marks

As observed when considering sub-rule 2(*i*), (*o*) and (*i*) are to some extent complementary. Similar considerations in relation to marks apply to this exception as apply to packing in sub-rule 2(*n*) in that the inadequacy cannot be one that was obvious on receipt/shipment. The most frequent use of this exception is not where the marks are inadequate, but where the marking is not properly accomplished and wears off with handling during the voyage, making identification difficult at destination.

(p) Latent defects not discoverable by due diligence

The exclusion of latent defect relates to defects in the ship and not the cargo (which is covered in sub-rule 2(*m*)). It is subject to the same test of due diligence as seaworthiness discussed in Article III, Rule 1 (*see* page 19), on each occasion when an inspection ought to be made. Latent defect may be described as a defect, which a competent person, examining according to the current standards prevalent in the trade, could not reasonably be expected to discover.

Latent defect is a flaw in the defective component and is not caused by corrosion or wastage, which ought to be discoverable by due diligence.

(q) Any other cause arising without the actual fault or privity of the carrier, or without the fault or neglect of the agents or servants of the carrier, but the burden of proof shall be on the person claiming the benefit of this exception to show that neither the actual fault or privity of the carrier nor the fault or neglect of the agents or servants of the carrier contributed to the loss or damage

This last exclusion has been described as the last resort of the rogue, but few defendants in cases involving the Hague/Hague-Visby Rules enter their pleas of defence without including it as an attempted catch-all. It appears to be invitingly wide, but few carriers have succeeded in discharging the onus of proof clearly placed upon them in this exclusion. Not only must the carrier show no negligence on his part, but he must show what the cause was and that it was not one in which his negligence was involved. Unexplained loss or damage will not suffice.

Rule 3

"The shipper shall not be responsible for loss or damage sustained by the carrier or the ship arising or resulting from any cause without the act, fault or neglect of the shipper, his agents or his servants."

The Rules are usually thought of as governing the liabilities of carriers. This Rule is a rare example of the Rules governing the liability of the shipper.

Whereas Article V permits the carrier to surrender any of the rights which he may claim pursuant to the Rules, no such latitude is allowed in respect of the shipper, who consequently cannot surrender these rights.

Rule 4

"Any deviation in saving or attempting to save life or property at sea or any reasonable deviation shall not be deemed to be an infringement or breach of these Rules or of the contract of carriage, and the carrier shall not be liable for any loss or damage resulting therefrom."

As was discussed when considering Article IV, Rule 2(*l*) (*see* page 37), a ship's master needs to be able to concentrate on giving assistance to other vessels in distress as part of the unwritten law of the sea, without having to worry about the effects of any actions he may take upon his liability to his shippers. Sub-rule 2(*l*) protects him from direct loss or damage thereby arising, whilst Rule 4 protects him from the effect of breach of the bill of lading contract by deviating from the most direct or advertised route of the voyage.

In addition, the carrier is protected in respect of "any reasonable deviation", but no guidance is given as to what is and is not reasonable. What is reasonable will always be a matter of fact and, as shipping practices change, what is reasonable will change also. What was unreasonable in break-bulk, port-to-port shipping may well be reasonable in containerised combined transport and, whilst there is some case law on the former, there is little or none on the latter.

Neither the Hague nor the Hague-Visby Rules deals with the concept of fundamental breach of contract directly. By implication there are five potential bases of fundamental breach:

  (a) Undeclared deck carriage.
  (b) Unreasonable deviation.
  (c) Misrepresentation relating to the goods by the shipper.
  (d) Gross negligence or wilful recklessness.
  (e) Delivery of cargo without production of bill of lading.

However, recent case law suggests that the courts are veering towards a rejection of this so-called legal doctrine which is more in line with modern requirements and the much changed modes of operation. Cases, such as *The Nea Tyhi (Parker Plywood Ltd.* v. *Nueva Fortuna Corporation of Liberia* [1982] 1 Lloyd's Rep. 606), in which Hague Rules limits were still applied in determining liability following unauthorised deck carriage, and *The Atlantic Saga* (Federal Court of Canada, 7 July 1983: *Schweizerische Metalwerke Selve and Co.* v. *A/B Svenska Amerika Linien and Atlantic Container Line Ltd.*), where a claim for delivery without production of bill of lading was actually time-barred in accordance with Article III, Rule 6, support this view.

This view is further supported in some very strong *obiter dicta* recorded by Kirby P. in the Supreme Court of New South Wales (Australia) Court of Appeal in April 1988 in *The Bunga Teratai* case *(Nissho Iwai Australia Ltd.* v. *Malaysian International Shipping Corp.)* where, in rejecting the appeal against Yeldham's decision in the Admiralty court in favour of the carrier, Kirby observed, *inter alia*:

"Secondly, there was no overt dispute that the flirtation of the common law with the so-called 'doctrine' of 'fundamental breach' of contracts is now over. . . . [in referring to the *Suisse Atlantique* decision] there was no doctrine of fundamental breach but only an obligation in each case for the court, construing the contract, to read the language and to secure from it the presumed intention of the parties. . . . In England, the *coup de grâce* to the 'doctrine' of fundamental breach, as a substantive rule of law, was administered by the House of Lords in *Photo Production Ltd.* v. *Securicor Transport Ltd.* [1980] A.C. 827".

When this is read in conjunction with the following remarks relating to judicial interpretation of contracts, it would seem that carriers have every chance of avoiding fundamental breach of contract if they put a suitable clause in their bill of lading contracts.

" . . . It takes those with the responsibility of construing commercial contracts back to the language by which the parties have chosen to express their agreement. Their duty is to give the words of the contract their ordinary meaning. It is to avoid strained constructions. If there is ambiguity, but only then, ambiguous words may be construed against the party which has proffered a written contract in standard form and in favour of the party to whom such a contract has been presented. But if the language of the written agreement clearly covers the eventualities which have occurred, that is an end of the matter. Elsewhere, and in a different context, I have expressed my views about the dangers that are involved if courts, without statutory warrant, substitute their opinions as to the adjustment of the commercial interests of the parties to a contract for those which the parties themselves have chosen to put in writing. . . . "

" . . . No court is authorised to bend and twist the language of such an agreement for the achievement of nationalistic, economic or other policies conceived to be desirable . . . "

Pretty stern stuff, particularly from a Court of Appeal and in an English law-based jurisdiction where such an *obiter dicta* is of substantial persuasive influence in an English court.

Thus, there is cause to think that the law in respect of deviation/fundamental breach of contract may be changing in favour of the carrier, as commercial practices change.

In any event, deviation is a point where the laws of different countries differ quite widely. If English law is changing in this regard, it is only to come into line with its continental counterpart, which takes a much more lenient view of deviation. US law is, if anything, even more strict and anti-carrier than its English equivalent and US courts remain the most unfavourable courts to carriers compared with European courts.

Accordingly, it may be seen that what is and is not a deviation is unclear. A "rule of thumb" used to be that anything done for the benefit of the whole venture (i.e. a general average type act) was not a deviation whereas any unscheduled deviation, such as to obtain cheap bunkers or load additional cargo, which was for the benefit of the carrier only, was a deviation. This is still quite an accurate way of determining what is not a deviation, but instances which fail this test may, in the light of recent development, not necessarily be a fundamental breach of contract.

The philosophy behind making deviation a fundamental breach of contract was that the cargo was thereby exposed to additional risks, to which its owner had not consented. For example, if a vessel proceeding down the Red Sea deviated to call at Jeddah to load additional cargo, the hazards of navigating into and out of Jeddah are additional unconsented risks. This was quite important in the days when some ports were poorly charted or uncharted and navigational aids were few and unreliable, but today, when most major ports are well charted and most vessels have sophisticated navigational aids, this importance shrinks into insignificance. Furthermore, in an era of combined transport utilising cellular containerships that are never empty, as they load concurrent with discharge, there are no clearly defined beginnings or ends to any voyage and loading/discharging itineraries, with/without feeding operations, have to be changed at the last moment to reflect changes in port conditions etc. This is all part of normal container shipping operation and it is so different from break-bulk operation that it can reasonably be claimed that break-bulk case law is, for the most, inapplicable and inappropriate to it. Thus, deviation is one area where a change in shipping practice is likely to bring about a change in case law interpretation of the Rules.

Rule 5

This is the Rule where the best recognised change was made by the Visby Amendments, in the limitation of liability. In the Hague Rules, Rule 5 reads:

"Neither the carrier nor the ship shall in any event be or become liable for any loss or damage to or in connection with goods in an amount exceeding 100 pounds sterling per package or unit, or the equivalent of that sum in other currency, unless the nature and value of such goods have been declared by the shipper before shipment and inserted in the bill of lading.

This declaration if embodied in the bill of lading shall be *prima facie* evidence, but shall not be binding or conclusive on the carrier.

By agreement between the carrier, master or agent of the carrier and the shipper another maximum amount than that mentioned in this paragraph may be fixed, provided that such maximum shall not be less than the figure above named.

Neither the carrier nor the ship shall be responsible in any event for loss or damage to or in connection with goods if the nature or value thereof has been knowingly misstated by the shipper in the bill of lading."

and this Rule has to be read in conjunction with Article IX of the Rules which reads:

"The monetary units mentioned in these Rules are to be taken to the gold value.

Those contracting States in which the pound sterling is not a monetary unit reserve to themselves the right of translating the sums indicated in this convention in terms of pound sterling into terms of their own monetary system in round figures.

The national laws may reserve to the debtor the right of discharging his debt in national currency according to the rate of exchange prevailing on the day of the arrival of the ship at the port of discharge of the goods concerned."

This is how Article IX read in the Hague Rules, but in the Schedule to COGSA 1924 only the first of the three paragraphs appears, the other two being deleted as being irrelevant, so far as the UK is concerned, as they cover details of the rights of states, where sterling is not the local currency, to exchange the limits into their own local currency.

At the time when the Hague Rules were drafted, the United Kingdom, in common with many other countries, was on the gold standard, that is to say that all currency issued was backed by gold to that value, so that one pound sterling was represented by one gold sovereign. When the United Kingdom came off the gold standard and inflation devalued the currency, arguments developed as to the correct amount of the package limitation in Rule 5. To obviate dispute on this point, British carriers and certain cargo interests and insurers entered into an agreement known as "The Gold Clause Agreement" (Article IX being known as the "Gold Clause"), by which British carriers agreed a limitation figure in pounds sterling currency with the other parties, initially £200 and later £400.

In passing Hague Rules legislation into their law, some nations adopted them as drafted, including the Rule 5 limitation in pounds sterling, which was the international measure of value of the day, rather as the US dollar is today. Those nations have had to face the Article IX "Gold Clause" problem and most have resolved it, without a form of agreement akin to the Gold Clause Agreement, by adopting gold value. However, most nations, in adopting or ratifying the Rules, translated Rule 5 into domestic currency as allowed in Article IX and amended Article IX, thereby avoiding "Gold Clause" problems. The limitations of the main Hague Rules maritime nations are (or were, before those marked * adopted Hague-Visby Rules):

*Australia	A$200	*New Zealand	NZ$200
*Canada	C$500	Portugal	ESC100,000
*Germany	DM1250	USA	US$500
*Greece	DR8000	USSR	R250
*Japan	Y100,000		

Although many nations still operate the Hague Rules, the fact that most European nations now apply the Hague-Visby Rules, and in particular the fact that the Hague-Visby Rules apply in the UK, resulted in the Gold Clause Agreement falling into disuse in June 1988. This coincided with a case in which a carrier tested the Gold Clause and (unsurprisingly) lost with the result that contractually applied Hague Rules now attracts a limit of over £6,600 per package (*The "Rosa S"* [1988] 2 Lloyd's Rep. 574). Fortunately for carriers this result is not disastrous, as most nations where Hague Rules are still mandatorily applicable have converted the package limitation into local currency instead of using the gold limitation. However, great care is needed in drafting bill of lading contracts (which usually contractually apply Hague Rules to shipments from those nations that have no mandatorily applicable law) to write in only Articles I to VIII of the Hague Rules and then provide separately for a package limitation of £100 (or whatever), thereby avoiding the "Gold Clause" trap.

To return to consideration of Rule 5. In paragraph 1 the Rule provides for the carrier to be able to limit his liability to £100 sterling per package or unit, unless the value of the goods is inserted in the bill of lading, thereby making it an *ad valorem* bill under which the value shown replaces the limitation provided in the Rule. Inevitably a shipper would pay a higher rate of freight for an *ad valorem* bill as the level of limitation is higher (*see* comment below re paragraph 3). In legislating to adopt the Hague Rules, the USA, not only changed the amount to US$500, but changed "per package or unit" to "per package or *customary freight unit*".

Thus, where goods were freighted as so much per ton instead of lump sum freight, the shipper had an option how to apply the limit—per package or per customary freight unit. Quite an important consideration with heavy lifts, such as railway engines, which carriers started to freight on a lump sum basis instead of per ton.

Palletisation and containerisation raised the question: what is the package—the pallet/container or the packages thereon/therein? The Hague-Visby Rules have dealt with this problem, so the question is only still valid in Hague Rules countries. Of these America has by far the greatest number of cases, with little consensus of opinion on the criteria to be established for a container to qualify as a package. The only decision in a north-west European court is a German decision which opined in favour of the container being a package. Given the guidance in the Hague-Visby Rules, this is surprising and it is generally felt that, if the court of a Hague-Visby country were, because of an appropriate jurisdiction clause, asked to litigate a case involving Hague Rules and this point were raised, the Hague-Visby interpretation would be applied and the number of packages shown in the bill of lading would be applied to determine limitation. (At the time of the German decision, German law still applied the Hague Rules.)

Paragraph 2 of Rule 5 provides that, where the bill is an *ad valorem* bill, the value shown is to be *prima facie* evidence only of the value of the goods. That is to say that the shipper is not relieved of the responsibility of proving the value of goods in the event of loss or damage, he merely has his level of recourse to the carrier increased. That it is increased and not decreased, in the event that the value stated is less than the package limitation provided in this Rule, is made clear in the third paragraph of this Rule, where declared values below the package limitation are made invalid.

The fourth and last paragraph of this Rule provides protection to the carrier where the shipper knowingly misstates the value or nature of the goods. This is the third potential basis for fundamental breach of contract discussed when considering Rule 4 (*see* page 40) and deprives a shipper of any recourse at all where the shipper is guilty of such a breach, even though he might, but for that breach, have had a valid claim against the carrier.

The Hague-Visby Rules Rule 5 reads:

"(a) Unless the nature and value of such goods have been declared by the shipper before shipment and inserted in the bill of lading, neither the carrier nor the ship shall in any event be or become liable for any loss or damage to or in connection with the goods in an amount exceeding the equivalent of 10,000 francs per package or unit of 30 francs per kilo of gross weight of the goods lost or damaged, whichever is the higher.

(b) The total amount recoverable shall be calculated by reference to the value of such goods at the place and time at which the goods are discharged from the ship in accordance with the contract or should have been so discharged.

   The value of the goods shall be fixed according to the commodity exchange price, or, if there be no such price, according to the current market price, or, if there be no commodity exchange price or current market price, by reference to the normal value of goods of the same kind and quality.

(c) Where a container, pallet or similar article of transport is used to consolidate goods, the number of packages or units enumerated in the bill of lading as packed in such article of transport shall be deemed the number of packages or units for the purpose of this paragraph as far as these packages or units are concerned. Except as aforesaid such article of transport shall be considered the package or unit.

(d) A franc means a unit consisting of 65.5 milligrammes of gold of millesimal fineness 900. The date of conversion of the sum awarded into national currencies shall be governed by the law of the Court seized of the case.

(e) Neither the carrier nor the ship shall be entitled to the benefit of the limitation of liability provided for in this paragraph if it is proved that the damage resulted from an act or omission of the carrier done with intent to cause damage, or recklessly and with knowledge that damage would probably result.

(f) The declaration mentioned in sub-paragraph (a) of this paragraph, if embodied in the bill of lading, shall be prima facie evidence, but shall not be binding or conclusive on the carrier.

(g) By agreement between the carrier, master or agent of the carrier and the shipper other maximum amounts than those mentioned in sub-paragraph (a) of this paragraph may be fixed, provided that no maximum amount so fixed shall be less than the appropriate maximum mentioned in that sub-paragraph.

(h) Neither the carrier nor the ship shall be responsible in any event for loss or damage to, or in connection with, goods if the nature or value thereof has been knowingly misstated by the shipper in the bill of lading."

and is clearly a much more detailed Rule than its Hague Rules counterpart,

"(a) Unless the nature and value of such goods have been declared by the shipper before shipment and inserted in the bill of lading, neither the carrier nor the ship shall in any event be or become liable for any loss or damage to or in connection with the goods in an amount exceeding the equivalent of 10,000 francs per package or unit of 30 francs per kilo of gross weight of the goods lost or damaged, whichever is the higher."

The limit in the Hague-Visby Rules incorporates a package/weight alternative, with whichever produces the higher limit being applicable. From the figures, it is possible to calculate that, where a package weighs less than 333.33 kilos, a package limit will be applied, but where it exceeds this weight a weight based limit is applicable. The limit is expressed in Poincaré francs, a fictitious measure of value which is defined in paragraph (d).

There is now in force a Protocol to the Hague-Visby Rules, which was signed at Brussels on 21 December 1979 and which is usually referred to as the 1979 Hague-Visby Special Drawing Rights (SDR) Protocol to differentiate it from another 1979 SDR Protocol relating to the 1957 Convention on Limitation of Liability (1958 MSA). This Protocol was given effect in the United Kingdom by the Merchant Shipping Act 1981 and substitutes limitation in SDRs for those in Poincaré francs in Rule 5 of the Hague-Visby Rules. In April 1997 the states applying this Protocol were:

Australia	Greece	Netherlands
Belgium	Hong Kong	New Zealand
Canada*	Iceland*	Norway
China*	Israel*	Poland
Denmark	Italy	Spain
Egypt*	Japan	Sweden
Finland	Liberia*	Switzerland
France	Luxembourg	United Kingdom
Germany*	Mexico	

* Applied by domestic legislation only

Thus, in the UK Act, Article IV, Rule 5(*a*) is amended to read:

> "(*a*) Unless the nature and value of such goods have been declared by the shipper before shipment and inserted in the bill of lading, neither the carrier nor the ship shall in any event be or become liable for any loss or damage to or in connection with the goods in an amount exceeding 666.67 units of account per package or unit or 2 units of account per kilogramme of gross weight of the goods lost or damaged, whichever is the higher."

(*See* also section 1, subsections (1) and (5), pages 9 and 10.)

The Protocol contains a provision to the effect that adoption of the Protocol constitutes adoption of the Hague-Visby Rules and Spain's application of the Hague-Visby Rules came about in this fashion without Spain having ratified or acceded to the Rules.

The advantage of having limitation expressed in SDRs, which is the mean of a basket of international currencies, is that conversion from SDRs to national currency is available by using data published in the financial press and is thus updated regularly and automatically. Poincaré francs, on the other hand, being fictitious currency, have no readily available conversion data. Thus, prior to the implementation of the SDR Protocol, it was necessary to issue frequent Orders in Council amending the sterling equivalent of the Poincaré franc limitations, as the fluctuation in the price of gold affected the value of the gold franc. This was a tedious business, which meant that practitioners were constantly in doubt as to the current value of limitation in sterling.

The SDR Hague-Visby limits are 2 SDRs per kilo or 666.67 SDRs per package. In August of 1997, 1 SDR was worth about US$1.37 (£0.82).

In relation to Poincaré francs it should be noted that, in English law, it is the rate of exchange/Order in Council prevalent at the time of settling the claim which applies and not the one prevalent at the date of loss or delivery, as it is this "rate of exchange" which puts the claimant in the position to purchase the requisite amount of the currency of limitation at the date of payment.

> "(b) The total amount recoverable shall be calculated by reference to the value of such goods at the place and time at which the goods are discharged from the ship in accordance with the contract or should have been so discharged.
>
> The value of the goods shall be fixed accordingly to the commodity exchange price, or, if there be no such price, according to the current market price, or, if there be no commodity exchange price or current market price, by reference to the normal value of goods of the same kind and quality."

This paragraph addresses itself to the problem of the basis of calculating loss rather than maximum limitation. The Hague Rules are silent on the point, but the principle of *restitutio in integrum*, i.c. that the claimant must be put back into the same position as he was in before loss or damage occurred, means that the basis of loss in the Hague Rules is sound market value for shortage and the difference between sound market value and damaged market value for damage. In the Hague-Visby Rules this paragraph goes into some detail setting this out but, in English law, because of the principle of *restitutio in integrum*, it creates no change from the Hague Rules position and does nothing to assist the shipper with his perennial problem of proving the quantum of his loss. Where there is a ready commodity market at the discharge port, no problems arise and some commodity associations issue regular schedules of sound market values of the different grades of goods which considerably assist in the settlement of claims. However, where no such ready market or commodity price lists exist, the shipper is frequently unable to prove anything other than c.i.f. value, which is often accepted by him because he is unable to discharge the onus upon him of proving the sound market value, to which he would be entitled if he could prove it.

> "(c) Where a container, pallet or similar article of transport is used to consolidate goods, the number of packages or units enumerated in the bill of lading as packed in such article of transport shall be deemed the number of packages or units for the purpose of this paragraph as far as these packages or units are concerned. Except as aforesaid such article of transport shall be considered the package or unit."

This paragraph answers the problem brought about by palletisation and containerisation to which reference was made earlier when considering the equivalent Rule to this in the Hague Rules (*see* page 44). It makes it quite clear what is the package for limitation purposes and, in this context, it is important to recognise that this applies to limitation only. Where a bill acknowledges "one container said to contain 500 packages", in the event of a claim, limitation is 500 × SDR 666.67, but in no way should it be thought that arrival of the sealed container with only 490 packages gives automatic recourse for 10 packages, as the carrier has not acknowledged 500 packages, but only one container *said to contain* 500 packages. The 500 applies to limitation only, not basis of liability. The only way a carrier under the Hague-Visby Rules can have the container regarded as a package is to acknowledge only "one container said to contain (say) wool", with no reference made on the bill to the number of bales. Even so, this would not enable him to limit on the basis of the container as a package, as the claimant would be entitled to the weight alternative, which would undoubtedly be higher in such circumstances.

> "(*d*) A franc means a unit consisting of 63.5 milligrammes of gold of millesimal fineness 900. The date of conversion of the sum awarded into national currencies shall be governed by the law of the Court seized of the case."

This paragraph defines Poincaré franc and provides for national law to govern the date of conversion into national currency. As observed earlier, in English law, this is the date of payment, but in any event Poincaré francs have been superseded by SDRs in the UK as a result of the adoption of the SDR Protocol by the Merchant Shipping Act 1981. This Act has changed this paragraph to read:

> "(*d*) The unit of account mentioned in this Article is the special drawing right as defined by the International Monetary Fund. The amounts mentioned in sub-paragraph (a) of this paragraph shall be converted into national currency on the basis of the value of that currency on a date to be determined by the law of the Court seized of the case."

thereby defining the unit of currency in which limitation is expressed in paragraph (*a*) as an SDR (*see* also section 1, subsections (1) and (5), pages 9 and 10).

It should be noted that there are differences in Article IV, Rule 5(*a*) and (*d*) between those nations that have adopted the SDR Protocol as well as the Visby amendment and those that have only adopted the Visby amendment.

> "(*e*) Neither the carrier nor the ship shall be entitled to the benefit of the limitation of liability provided for in this paragraph if it is proved that the damage resulted from an act or omission of the carrier done with intent to cause damage, or recklessly and with knowledge that damage would probably result."

This is the fourth potential basis for fundamental breach of contract discussed when considering Rule 4 (*see* page 40). It is in line with the requirement in the 1976 Convention on Limitation of Liability for Maritime Claims for being able to apply limitation under the Merchant Shipping Acts. It almost equates to criminal negligence and creates a situation where limitation is denied only in the most extreme cases.

Note that this paragraph only provides for breach of limitation and does not entitle the claimant to avoid the time bar under Article III, Rule 6 (*see* page 26) which continues to operate in respect of . . . "all liability whatsoever".

"(*f*) The declaration mentioned in sub-paragraph (*a*) of this paragraph, if embodied in the bill of lading, shall be prima facie evidence, but shall not be binding or conclusive on the carrier."

This paragraph is identical to paragraph 2 of Rule 5 of the Hague Rules (*see* pages 42 and 45).

"(*g*) By agreement between the carrier, master or agent of the carrier and the shipper other maximum amounts than those mentioned in sub-paragraph (*a*) of this paragraph may be fixed, provided that no maximum amount so fixed shall be less than the appropriate maximum mentioned in that sub-paragraph."

This paragraph is similar in effect to paragraph 3 of Rule 5 of the Hague Rules (*see* pages 42 and 45), the only differences being those of drafting necessary to accommodate the alternative package/weight limits of the Hague-Visby Rules compared to the package only limit of the Hague Rules.

"(*h*) Neither the carrier nor the ship shall be responsible in any event for loss or damage to, or in connection with, goods if the nature or value thereof has been knowingly misstated by the shipper in the bill of lading."

This paragraph is identical to paragraph 4 of Rule 5 of the Hague Rules (*see* pages 42 and 45).

Rule 6

This Rule is identical in both sets of Rules and provides that:

"Goods of an inflammable, explosive or dangerous nature to the shipment whereof the carrier, master or agent of the carrier has not consented with knowledge of their nature and character, may at any time before discharge be landed at any place, or destroyed or rendered innocuous by the carrier without compensation and the shipper of such goods shall be liable for all damages and expenses directly or indirectly arising out of or resulting from such shipment. If any such goods shipped with such knowledge and consent shall become a danger to the ship or cargo, they may in like manner be landed at any place, or destroyed or rendered innocuous by the carrier without liability on the part of the carrier except to general average, if any."

These wide powers are very necessary to the carrier, even more so today than when they were first penned, with cargoes of highly toxic substances frequently being moved. The advent of containers giving goods anonymity, which is a useful aid against theft, also brings increased fears that somewhere, probably in a container packed by an inexperienced groupage agent, will be two incompatible undeclared hazardous cargoes, which will react and cause a disaster of unparalleled proportions. Many carriers make special checks on all or a high proportion of hazardous and groupage boxes in an effort to prevent this. Shipping has already had one such disaster with "Asiafreighter", in which arsine gas (a gaseous form of arsenic) escaped with disastrous consequences. It is anxious to avoid a repetition.

ARTICLE IV: *BIS*

This article (as the *bis* suggests) is solely a Hague-Visby Rules provision. It contains some useful and interesting amendments added in the light of experience with the Hague Rules.

Rule 1

"The defences and limits of liability provided for in these Rules shall apply in any action against the carrier in respect of loss or damage to goods covered by a contract of carriage whether the action be founded in contract or in tort."

This is quite an interesting addition. It was once thought that only a bill of lading holder could claim against a carrier as any other party would be too remote for the carrier to owe him a duty of care. If this were so then, as the Hague-Visby Rules only apply where a bill of lading is issued, this Rule would be superfluous, as there would be no tortious claims. In *The Irene's Success (Schiffahrt-und-Kohlen GmbH* v *Chelsea Maritime Ltd.)* [1981] 2 Lloyd's Rep. 635, the High Court decided that the carrier owed a duty of care to the holder of a delivery order. In *The Aliakmon (Leigh and Sillivan Ltd.* v. *Aliakmon Shipping Co.)* [1986] 2 All E.R. 145, the House of Lords confirmed the traditional and contrary view. A court outside the UK may take a different view so Rule 1 may yet prove useful to some carrier, provided that he has issued a bill of lading somewhere along the line, as the Rule only applies in respect of claims on cargo for which a contract of carriage in the form of a bill of lading has been issued.

Rule 2

"If such an action is brought against a servant or agent of the carrier (such servant or agent not being an independent contractor), such servant or agent shall be entitled to avail himself of the defences and limits of liability which the carrier is entitled to invoke under these Rules."

This is the incorporation into the Hague-Visby Rules of two-thirds of the protection of the "Himalaya" clause, drafted to protect servants, agents and sub-contractors from tortious action, by claimants seeking to circumvent the limitations in the contract of carriage, by giving them the benefit of the contract. Where the Hague-Visby Rules apply, the "Himalaya" clause (so-called after the vessel upon which the party, whose counsel identified the loophole that the clause was designed to plug, travelled) is now superfluous, so far as servants and agents are concerned, but still needs to be retained to protect sub-contractors. The "Himalaya" case was *Adler* v. *Dickson* [1955] 1 Q.B. 158, where Mrs Adler avoided an indemnity in her passage ticket against claims for personal injury by suing the captain instead in tort.

Rule 3

"The aggregate of the amounts recoverable from the carrier, and such servants and agents, shall in no case exceed the limit provided for in these Rules."

Claimants have been known to attempt two "bites at the cherry" by arranging for both shipper and consignee to claim. This clause precludes such sharp practice.

Rule 4

"Nevertheless, a servant or agent of the carrier shall not be entitled to avail himself of the provisions of this article, if it is proved that the damage resulted from an act or omission of the servant or agent done with intent to cause damage or recklessly and with knowledge that damage would probably result."

This Rule applies the same sanction on servants and agents as Article IV, Rule 5(*e*), applies to the carrier who is guilty of such misdemeanors (*see* pages 42 and 45).

ARTICLE V: SURRENDER OF RIGHTS AND IMMUNITIES AND INCREASE OF RESPONSIBILITIES AND LIABILITIES

"A carrier shall be at liberty to surrender in whole or in part all or any of his rights and immunities or to increase any of his responsibilities and obligations under these Rules, provided such surrender or increase shall be embodied in the bill of lading issued to the shipper. The provisions of these Rules shall not be applicable to charterparties, but if bills of lading are issued in the case of a ship under a charterparty they shall comply with the terms of these Rules. Nothing in these Rules shall be held to prevent the insertion in a bill of lading of any lawful provision regarding general average."

This article, which is common to both the Hague Rules and the Hague-Visby Rules, covers three points:

(a)   The ability of the carrier to apply terms more favourable to the shipper than those provided in the Rules.

(b)   Bills issued pursuant to charterparties.

(c)   General average.

(a) The Rules are designed as the minimum basis upon which a carrier can contract with a shipper for the carriage of goods and are not intended to restrict carriers from offering more generous terms, albeit usually at greater cost, as in the case of *ad valorem* bills, to which reference was made when discussing Article IV, Rule 5 (*see* pages 42 and 45). However, where a carrier does so, the Rules require him to incorporate the details of the more favourable terms in the bill of lading contract.

(b) Charterparties are not mandatorily subject to the Rules, bills of lading are. Thus if a charterparty incorporates terms which are repugnant to the Rules then, as between carrier and charterer, those terms are enforceable and any bill issued by the carrier to the charterer acts as a receipt only, with the charterparty being the contract of carriage. However, if the charterer negotiates that bill to an innocent third party purchaser for value, even though the bill incorporates the terms of the charterparty, the contract of carriage between the new owner of the goods and the carrier now becomes the bill of lading and the charterparty terms and conditions are only applicable to the extent that they are not repugnant to the Rules.

(c) The Rules make no attempt to govern general average (*see* Appendix III, page 111), but merely allow it to be provided for in bills of lading. As it is not a written law, bills need to make provision for its adjustment, usually in accordance with the York-Antwerp Rules, the latest version being the 1994 Rules agreed at the Comité Maritime International Conference in Sydney in October 1994. (*See* Appendix III page 111.)

ARTICLE VI: SPECIAL CONDITIONS

"Notwithstanding the provisions of the preceding articles, a carrier, master or agent of the carrier and a shipper shall in regard to any particular goods be at liberty to enter into any agreement in any terms as to the responsibility and liability of the carrier for such goods, and as to the rights and immunities of the carrier in respect of such goods, or his obligation as to seaworthiness, so far as this stipulation is not contrary to public policy, or the care or diligence of his servants or agents in regard to the loading, handling, stowage, carriage, custody, care and discharge of the goods carried by sea, provided that in this case no bill of lading has been or shall be issued and that the terms agreed shall be embodied in a receipt which shall be a non-negotiable document and shall be marked as such.

Any agreement so entered into shall have full legal effect.

Provided that this article shall not apply to ordinary commercial shipments made in the ordinary course of trade, but only to other shipments where the character or condition of the property to be carried or the circumstances, terms and conditions under which the carriage is to be performed are such as reasonably to justify a special agreement."

This article is also common to both sets of Rules. It provides for a carrier to be free to contract upon any terms, even though contrary to the Rules, for the carriage of cargo which may be regarded as not being an "ordinary commercial shipment" provided that he issues a non-negotiable document (i.e. not a bill of lading) as the contract of carriage.

In his Meredith Memorial Lecture of 1982, Professor William Tetley, Q.C., makes out a case for the Hague and Hague-Visby Rules being mandatorily applicable to waybills, even though they are not a "similar document of title". This is based on, what Professor Tetley calls, "the public order nature of the Hague Rules", that is to say that they are mandatory law for contracting for the carriage of goods by sea. This overlooks the fact that application of the Rules is inextricably linked to documents of title and there really is no reason in law why a waybill should be set alongside a bill of lading rather than an NNR or charterparty. Nevertheless, this potential dispute is academic rather than real, as most waybills voluntarily incorporate bill of lading conditions and warrant that these incorporate the Hague/Hague-Visby Rules. Furthermore, the Uniform Rules for Sea Waybills, which the Comité Maritime International adopted at their 1990 conference in Paris, also offer a potential solution to this problem. (*See* Part 4 page 73.)

General guidance is given in the third paragraph as to what type of shipments qualify for this article and these are generally interpreted as including the following:

Personal effects.

Household effects.

Secondhand cars.

Experimental shipments (i.e. a new cargo regarding which outturn is uncertain, particularly a refrigerated cargo or one being carried under special conditions, such as a new type of packing).

and there will come a time, after successful carriage for a period, when experimental shipments cease to be experimental and become normal, as knowledge and expertise is acquired. The Unfair Contract Terms Act specifically does not apply to contracts for the carriage of goods by sea, so there is no conflict between this article and that Act. However, the Act does apply to contracts for the carriage of goods by land, so, where combined transport is involved, carriers often elect not to take advantage of this article and leave themselves open to a possibility of breach of the Act during the land leg and elect, instead, to issue a bill of lading (or waybill giving identical recourse). Accordingly, non-negotiable receipts (NNRs) are much less used nowadays in the UK based trades.

Note the difference in the treatment of live animals, deck cargo and non-commercial shipments. With live animals the carrier can avoid liability under the Rules without clausing the bill of lading (but where Hague-Visby is involved he must make clear his intention not to apply the Rules to live animals in his terms and conditions). With deck cargo he can avoid the Rules by clausing the bill accordingly. In the case of both live animals and deck cargo, therefore, a bill may be issued. However, with non-commercial shipments, if a carrier wishes to avoid the Rules, he must avoid issuing a bill and instead issue a non-negotiable document.

ARTICLE VII: LIMITATIONS ON THE APPLICATION OF THE RULES

"Nothing herein contained shall prevent a carrier or a shipper from entering into any agreement, stipulation, condition, reservation or exemption as to the responsibility and liability of the carrier or the ship for the loss or damage to, or in connection with, the custody and care and handling of goods prior to the loading on, and subsequent to, the discharge from the ship on which the goods are carried by sea."

This article, which is also identical in both sets of Rules, emphasises that the Rules only cover from loading up to discharge. However, if the carrier wishes to contract on terms outside the Rules at these times, he should do so expressly. In *Pyrene Co. Ltd.* v. *Scindia Steam Navigation Co.* [1954] 1 Lloyd's Rep. 321, it was held that, where the contract requires the carrier to undertake the loading and/or discharging operations, the Rules are applicable to these operations. In relation to any given consignment, it was established in *Goodwin Ferreira & Co. Ltd.* v. *Lamport and Holt Ltd.* (1929) 34 Ll.L.R. 192 that a consignment is not discharged until the whole consignment is discharged.

In America, the Harter Act of 1893 preceded the US COGSA 1936 and covered the period prior to loading and after discharge. When the US COGSA 1936 was enacted, the Harter Act remained in force to cover these periods and was only repealed by the US COGSA 1936 so far as sea carriage is concerned. Thus, under American law, this article is not operational.

ARTICLE VIII: LIMITATION OF LIABILITY

"The provisions of these Rules shall not affect the rights and obligations of the carrier under any statute for the time being in force relating to the limitation of the liability of owners of seagoing vessels."

This article is common to both sets of Rules and is duplicated in the introductory clauses of both Acts, in section 6(2) of the COGSA 1924 and section 6(4) of the COGSA 1971, where more specific reference is made to the appropriate UK Merchant Shipping Acts (*see* pages 4 *et seq.* for comment).

ARTICLE IX: GOLD CLAUSE/NUCLEAR EXCLUSION

Article IX in the Hague Rules is quite different to Article IX in the Hague-Visby Rules.

Reference has already been made to Article IX of the Hague Rules when considering Article IV, Rule 5 (*see* page 42) and further comment is unnecessary, Article IX of the Hague-Visby Rules reads:

"These Rules shall not affect the provisions of any international Convention or national law governing liability for nuclear damage."

This article is, perhaps, a sign of the times, in as much as nuclear damage was an unheard of horror when the Hague Rules were drafted. It is merely a recognition that there are international Conventions and national laws relating to nuclear damage and recognises that these take precedence over the Rules.

ARTICLE X: APPLICATION

In the Hague Rules this Article reads:

"The provisions of this convention shall apply to all bills of lading issued in any of the contracting States."

This article does not form part of the Schedule to COGSA 1924, which terminates with Article IX, and instead sections 1 and 4 of the introductory clauses deal with the matter by applying different criteria (*see* page 1), namely that the Rules apply to shipments from UK ports, subject to the provisions of those two sections, rather than to bills of lading issued in the UK.

In the Hague-Visby Rules this article reads:

"The provisions of these Rules shall apply to every bill of lading relating to the carriage of goods between ports in two different States if:
(*a*) the bill of lading is issued in a contracting State, or
(*b*) the carriage is from a port in a contracting State, or
(*c*) the contract contained in or evidenced by the bill of lading provides that these Rules or legislation of any State giving effect to them are to govern the contract.
whatever may be the nationality of the ship, the carrier, the shipper, the consignee, or any other interested person."

As may be seen, the Hague-Visby Rules apply the criteria of the Hague Rules and the COGSA 1971 as options (*a*) and (*b*) as well as a third option (*c*), of which more later.

The fact that some nations apply the Hague-Visby Rules whilst others still apply the Hague Rules creates some complications, which are further exacerbated by the growth of combined transport. Consider, for instance, the case of a shipment from Switzerland (a Hague-Visby Rules nation) to, say, Australia. The shipment may go via Rotterdam (Holland is Hague-Visby Rules) or Lisbon (Portugal is Hague Rules). If it is shipped via Rotterdam, no problem, Hague-Visby Rules are applicable (paragraph (*b*) applies), but, if it is shipped via Lisbon, it depends on where the bill is issued. If it is issued in Lisbon, Hague Rules apply, whereas if it is issued in Switzerland, Hague-Visby Rules apply. Undesirable scope thus exists for manoeuvring.

Note that (*a*) refers to where a bill is "issued". This raises the point: where is a bill issued? Where it is produced/signed or where it is handed to the shipper, which may not be one and the same place? Many bills avoid this problem by showing where they are issued as part of the signature clause at the foot of the face of the bill. For the rest, it is not a point which appears to have arisen so far, and particularly now that many bills are carrier-produced and posted to shippers, it seems likely that the place of issue would be regarded as the place where the bill was produced and signed.

Paragraph (*c*) is interesting and has been the subject of some debate. It provides for the Rules to apply:

(i) if the Bill of Lading contractually imports them; and
(ii) if the Bill of Lading provides to incorporate the legislation of any state giving effect to them.

It has been suggested that an English law and jurisdiction clause in a bill of lading is sufficient contractually to apply the Hague-Visby Rules, as the UK has given effect to the Rules. Unfortunately for the recovery agents who have put forward this suggestion, it does not stand up to closer examination. This would only be so if the law of England provided for *all* contracts of carriage of goods by sea to be subject to the COGSA 1971. It does not so provide and instead stipulates that criteria (*a*) (*b*) or (*c*) must first be satisfied. So, effectively, if criterion (*a*) or (*b*) is not satisfied the Rules do not apply, unless criterion (*c*) is met and an English law clause does not do this, all English law does is to apply criterion (*c*) to determine whether or not the Rules are applicable. The argument is, thus, wholly circular and fails to clear the hurdle of onus of proof that COGSA 1971 applies.

Note that the preamble to Article X provides for the Rules to apply only "to the carriage of goods between ports in two different States". In the case of COGSA 1971 this is contravened by section 1(3) (*see* page 9). Thus, in so far as COGSA 1971 is concerned, sections 1(3) and (6) of the Act need to be read in conjunction with Article X to obtain the true meaning, as the Act amends the Schedule somewhat.

ARTICLES XI XVI

The Rules have 16 articles. Only the first nine (with curtailment of Article IX) are reproduced as a Schedule to COGSA 1924 and the first 10 as a Schedule to COGSA 1971.

Articles XI to XVI are not produced and commented upon here as they do not cover matters relating to carriers' liabilities and merely cover:

   (i)   the coming into force of the Convention,
  (ii) procedure for ratification, accession and denunciation, and
 (iii) the right to call for a fresh conference to consider amendments to the Rules contained in the Convention.

PART 2

GENERAL AVERAGE AND SALVAGE

GENERAL AVERAGE

General average is an unwritten international maritime law, which is universally recognised and applied. It has been practised since time immemorial and was part of the Rhodian law. It is founded on the principle that ship and goods are parties to the same venture and share exposure to the same perils, which may require sacrifice on the part of one, or the incurring of extraordinary expense, for the benefit of the whole venture.

A general average may be either a sacrifice or an expenditure, but in order to qualify as such it must satisfy ALL of the following criteria. It must be:

(i) extraordinary in nature (normal expense or damage is excluded);
(ii) voluntarily,
(iii) deliberately (accidental damage is excluded—i.e. particular average),
(iv) and reasonably incurred;
(v) in time of general peril (the whole venture, i.e. ship and cargo, must be threatened);
(vi) for the common safety (expense aimed at saving only part of the venture is excluded);
(vii) of a maritime nature (general average is peculiar to maritime ventures);
(viii) the danger must be real (imagined danger does not qualify);
(ix) and imminent (expenses foreseeing and avoiding danger do not qualify (i.e. deviation to avoid a storm) as this is part of the carrier's normal expense/responsibility);
(x) and must succeed in saving some part of the venture (otherwise nothing is left to contribute!).

Each of these requirements is essential and, if one is missing, the sacrifice or expense involved is not allowable in general average. General average is then the process by which those parties to the venture, whose interests have been sacrificed or who have incurred extra expense, are recompensed by the contribution of those whose interests have been saved.

Typical examples of general average sacrifices are jettison to lighten a grounded ship in order to float-off and water damage to goods from attempts to extinguish a fire. General average expenses can be port of refuge expenses where a ship puts into an unscheduled port for essential repairs to complete the voyage.

When a general average occurs, a specialist firm of average adjusters is appointed to assist with the initial problems and calculate the contribution due from each interest. Ship, containers, goods and unearned freight will contribute according to their market value. The first problem is to obtain security for general average contribution from cargo interests, because the adjustment may take years before it is issued. This is achieved by obtaining the merchant's signature on an average bond (the promise to pay), which is backed by either an average guarantee signed by a reputable underwriter, or by a cash deposit based on the contributing value estimated by the average adjuster.

Although the principle of general average is a generally accepted unwritten law, the practical application of it and the preparation of the adjustment could give rise to disagreement in the absence of written guidelines. In modern times these have been provided by the Comité Maritime International, who publish Rules governing general average known as the York-Antwerp Rules. Not being law, it is necessary to incorporate these Rules into contracts of carriage by specific mention therein. The Rules are periodically reviewed and revised in the light of changing requirements and circumstances. The presently applicable version is the York-Antwerp Rules 1994.

There is a growing tendency these days for cargo interests to contest general average contribution on the ground of unseaworthiness as, if the cargo interest can show that the carrier is in breach of his obligation under Article III, Rule 1, he can avoid responsibility to contribute. This, along with the high cost of average adjusters' fees, has persuaded some liner operators that general average should be avoided whenever practicable. Accordingly, many have entered into agreements with their hull insurers to pay small general averages in full, on the basis that ship's proportion of contribution, with a costly adjustment involving a large number of bills of lading, is frequently as much as the entire general average expense without an adjustment.

Any party who has incurred a general average expense or suffered a general average loss or damage may declare general average, exercise a lien on ship and cargo and call for contribution. However, as few general averages relate to loss or damage without expense, and as the expense is almost invariably initially incurred by the ship operator, it is usually the ship owner that declares general average but charterers, as contracting carriers may sometimes do so.

Although reference is made to general average in bills of lading, it is an entirely separate contract from the contract of carriage. For example, consider a shipment on a chartered vessel under a bill of lading issued by the charterer to a third party which has no demise clause (*see* page 15). The ship operator is not in contract with the cargo owner and is not a party to the bill of lading contract but he may declare general average and call for contribution from the cargo owner. What is more, despite what is in the charterer's bill of lading, he is not obliged to apply the York-Antwerp Rules 1994, 1974, 1950 or any other version and can opt for his own choice of general average rules, unless the charterer has restricted him to a particular edition of the York-Antwerp Rules by a clause in the charterparty (as any prudent charterer would). The Russians and Chinese have their own version of general average rules, which are very similar to the York-Antwerp Rules and Rhine vessels often use the Rhine Rules.

SPECIAL CHARGES

Charges incurred solely for the benefit of individual consignments of cargo as opposed to the whole venture (i.e. ship and cargo) are special charges and are chargeable to the consignment(s) concerned and do not form part of the general average expenses, except to the extent that they inflate the difference between sound and damaged values of cargo damaged by a general average act which affects the level of contribution. (Special charges are sometimes referred to as particular charges.)

SALVAGE

In addition (or alternatively) to a ship in distress incurring extraordinary expense or making deliberate sacrifice in the interest of the whole venture and declaring general average, it may occur that a ship in distress receives assistance from a third party to assist to save the adventure. Another ship may tow a powerless ship to a place of safety, assist in extinguishing a fire or render some other service valuable to the ship and its cargo. In such circumstances that other ship is entitled to claim salvage from the ship and its cargo once it has completed valuable service and it is entitled to exercise a lien on the ship and its cargo for its salvage reward.

Salvage is frequently (but not always) undertaken on the basis of "No Cure–No Pay" subject to Lloyd's Open Form of Salvage Agreement, the latest version being LOF 95 (*see* Appendix IV). Under this arrangement the salvor only gets paid if he succeeds in saving the ship and its cargo (or some part thereof). If LOF 95 is used, security for salvage (often in addition to security for general average) must be lodged with Lloyd's in London by a London-based acceptable security (usually a cargo insurer or his London agent for cargo and a hull insurer for the ship) to secure release of ship and cargo, although salvors may agree to alternative arrangements if they want the salvage arbitration heard elsewhere. If more than one salvor is involved separate security for each salvor may be necessary.

Salvage is not necessarily rendered only by other ships. For example containers washed overboard or floating off a stricken ship which come ashore may be salved by land-based salvors using land-based gear. In such cases the same principles apply but it is unlikely that any LOF 95 agreement will be used.

Salvage is assessed by an arbitrator and adjusted by an average adjuster, in the same way as (and often along with) general average.

STOP PRESS: Following the final House of Lords decision in the *Nagasaki Spirit* award (in which the interpretation of Article 14 was held not to include a profit element) salvors are unhappy with the current position and their trade association, the ISU (International Salvage Union), is in discussion with the P&I clubs through their IPG (International Pool Group) with a view to producing a revised "Salvage 2000", primarily to overcome the present repugnant interpretation of Article 14 of the 1989 Salvage Convention/LOF 95.

CONCLUSION

The essential difference between general average and salvage is that general average involves voluntary sacrifice or expense BY A PARTY TO THE VENTURE whereas salvage involves assistance by a THIRD PARTY INDEPENDENT OF CONTRACT to the venture in order to save it (or part of it) in time of peril.

PART 3

COUNTRIES APPLYING A VARIATION OF HAGUE RULES AND HAGUE-VISBY RULES AND CURRENT DEVELOPMENTS (AS AT AUGUST 1997)

AUSTRALIA

There has always been strong pressure on the Australian Government from the Australian Peak Shippers Association (APSA) to opt for the Hamburg Rules despite the competitive pressures of stepping out of line with (and thereby being in conflict with) their major trading partners and competitors (especially their Commonwealth partners in New Zealand, Canada and South Africa). This led to a "Hamburg poison pill" being added to the Australian COGSA 1991, which came into operation in November 1991 to apply the Hague-Visby Rules plus SDR Protocol, whereby Hamburg Rules would automatically come into operation in November 1994 unless Parliament passed legislation to the contrary beforehand. In October 1994 legislation postponing the "trigger" for a further three years was enacted and the Department of Transport set up a discussion group to try to resolve the conflicting views of merchants and carriers (it now being fairly obvious that Hamburg Rules were generally unacceptable and unlikely to attract support from major trading nations).

In July 1996 the Australian Department of Transport and Regional Development issued an information paper outlining the findings of its Cargo Liability Working Group in the following terms:

"The Cargo Liability Working Group, noting that the Minister for Transport has stated that the Hamburg Rules remain the preferred longer term approach for Australia, and that shippers favour a move to the Hamburg Rules as soon as possible, also recognised that carriers favour the continuation of the current Amended Hague Rules regime but are willing to support a modernisation of that regime. The Cargo Liability Working Group considered at length the elements of difference on which a compromise is achievable, and offered proposals for consideration by the industry.

A meeting of industry interests endorsed the following proposals (which differ slightly from the Proposal in the report in respect of non-negotiable documents, value limits and the time bar) as the basis for recommendations to the Minister for Transport:

1. That the *Carriage of Goods by Sea Act* 1991 ('the Act') be amended in the following respects:

Non-negotiable documents:
All relevant shipping documents should be covered, including electronic documents. The coverage by the Carriage of Goods by Sea Act of non-negotiable documents in the coastal trades will be further considered.

Deck cargo:
Deck cargo be covered by the liability regime, provided that, no later than the time of booking, the specific stowage requirements of the shipper have been notified to and agreed by the carrier.

Duration of liability:
Carrier liability be extended to the period where the cargo is in the carrier's care within the limits of the wharf or terminal at port of loading and discharge.

Arbitration:
There should be explicit provision for arbitration in the Act. A reference to arbitration in Australia should not constitute an ouster of jurisdiction offending Section 11.

Coverage of Importers:
The Carriage of Goods by Sea Act should specify that, where the contract of carriage does not incorporate one of the international conventions, importers' contracts of carriage are covered by the international convention in force in the Act.

Delays:
Carriers be made liable for loss due to delay, to the Hamburg Rules limit of 2.5 times the freight payable on the goods delayed, except where the delay is an 'excusable delay'.

2. That, in the interests of international uniformity, Australia actively support, in relevant international forums, the widespread adoption of a modernised cargo liability regime, compatible with the elements in 1., and also to reflect the following additional elements:

Nautical fault:
Providing there is clear international support for such a move by Australia's major trading partners, Australia also support abolition or partial abolition of the nautical fault defence, at least in respect of act, neglect or default in the management of the ship as a basis for an exemption from liability.

Value limits:
The Hamburg Rules limits be adopted for loss or damage to goods.

Time Bar:
A two-year time bar, together with a period of notice, as per the Hamburg Rules.

3. Given that under this approach some changes will be made to the Act, and that Australia will actively support international efforts towards a more uniform regime, the continuation of the trigger mechanism in the current legislation seems unnecessary. It is proposed that the trigger be repealed at the time the amendments proposed in 1. above are implemented, and before the next scheduled consideration of this mechanism in 1997, and be replaced by a mechanism for regular review of the international situation regarding the Hamburg Rules."

An amending Act entitled the Carriage of Goods by Sea Amendment Act 1997 was passed by the House of Representatives in June 1997 and Senate ratification in September 1997 brought the Act into effect on 15th September 1997 to repeal the "trigger" mechanism. The rest of the provisions of the Act were at that time not drafted and will be implemented by way of regulation in due course.

The Act provides for reviews at least every five years by the Minister to determine whether Hamburg Rules be adopted and, whilst precise criteria are not provided, the Minister has to take the following into account;

(a) to consider the extent to which the Hamburg Rules have been adopted internationally, in particular by Australia's major trading partners; and

(b) to consult with representatives of shippers, ship owners, carriers, cargo owners, marine insurers and maritime law associations on the question whether the amended Hague Rules should be replaced by the Hamburg Rules.

However, if after 10 years after the commencement of the new Act no option for Hamburg Rules is declared, the threat of Hamburg Rules is removed by the automatic repeal of that provision in the Act.

CANADA

In May 1993 the Canadian Parliament enacted legislation applying Hague-Visby Rules plus SDR Protocol with a "Hamburg poison pill" similar to that which Australia is just adopting i.e. subject to review by the Minister at least every six years. No criteria are established but it is generally understood that the approach of major trading partners will carry substantial influence. It is generally assumed that Australian "borrowed" this idea from Canada.

CHINA

In July 1993 China published a Maritime Code covering most maritime legal requirements and in many cases following (broadly) current international conventions on the subject matter concerned. Chapter IV of the Code deals with Contracts of Carriage of Goods by Sea and many of the provisions of this chapter are based on the Hague-Visby Rules plus SDR Protocol.

Points to note are as follows:

1. Carrier is liable for unreasonable delay—limited to the freight for the goods. Notice must be given in 60 days.

2. Period of responsibility is normal Hague-Visby for uncontainerised goods but from receipt at port of loading to delivery at port of discharge if containerised.

3. Notice of claim period is seven days for uncontainerised and 15 days if containerised.

Nothing is certain in Chinese courts. There are nine maritime courts in China and no reporting system so none know what the others are doing, thereby leading to conflicting decisions and worrying inconsistency. One court recently held that time extensions agreed between the parties were invalid and time barred a claim for which an extension had been agreed.

The Maritime Code Chapter IV refers to foreign trade only (not coastal) and China has not ratified or acceded to the relevant international conventions.

EGYPT

Egypt is a signatory to the Hamburg Rules but has exercised a right under Article 31(4) of those Rules to defer denunciation of Hague-Visby Rules for five years. As a result Hamburg Rules do not become effective in Egypt until 1 November 1998 and Egypt continues to apply Hague-Visby Rules plus SDR Protocol until then.

GERMANY

Being the host nation for the diplomatic conference that produced the Hamburg Rules made it too embarrassing for Germany to ratify or accede to any alternative Rules. They got around the problem by not ratifying or acceding to either Hague-Visby or Hamburg Rules but by merely adjusting their Commercial Code to apply Hague-Visby as their preferred choice.

INDIA

In October 1992, whilst Parliament was in recess, India enacted its Multimodal Transportation of Goods Ordinance by Presidential decree. Its declared aim was to promote combined transport within India. Its effect, if ever enforced, will be to ensure that combined transport dies and carriers revert to port-to-port shipping.

The main part of the Act sets out to regulate multimodal transport operators by licensing and, *inter alia*, seeks to provide for a liability regime heavily based on the UNCTAD Multimodal Convention, a set of Rules so unacceptable that most carriers will do anything to avoid them.

Part II of the Schedule to the Act amends the Indian Carriage of Goods by Sea Act 1925 to apply the Hague-Visby Rules plus SDR Protocol so that these apply to port-to-port shipping, thereby providing a massive incentive to carriers to avoid multimodal contracts and instead restrict themselves to a series of unimodal contracts only in order to obtain more reasonable contract of carriage terms. This would undoubtedly have led to "through B/L" type liabilities with carriers being principals at sea subject to COGSA but agent only on land liable to what was recoverable from Indian Railways or the haulier, not an attractive proposition!

Having realised that they had "shot themselves in the foot" (so to speak) the Indians adopted their time honoured face saving posture of not admitting to error (few politicians do!) but merely "sidelined" the legislation and ignored it whilst they decided how they could quietly resolve the predicament into which they had precipitated themselves! Political upheaval in the sub-continent has meant that more pressing matters have engaged the attention of the government so we find ourselves in an uncertain state of limbo where India is concerned.

Is the main part of the Act covering multimodal operations operative or not? If not then is the Schedule updating COGSA 25 to Hague-Visby plus SDR Protocol effective? Only an Indian court can tell us and to get there for a decision could take 10 years.

In the circumstances the only advice possible is avoid Indian law and jurisdiction in maritime contracts of carriage.

JAPAN

Be aware that Japanese COGSA provides for the carrier to be liable for delay in certain circumstances. Otherwise the Act is Hague-Visby plus SDR Protocol.

KOREA (SOUTH)

The Revised Commercial Code (RCC) replaced the Korean Commercial Code of 1962 (KCC) on 1 January 1993. It is mainly based on the Hague-Visby Rules. The main differences are:
1. It is the contracting carrier rather than the shipowner who is primarily liable under the Bill of Lading contract (i.e. escape via Identity of Carrier Clause prohibited).
2. The limit of liability is SDRs 500 with no weight alternative.

SCANDINAVIA

The Scandinavian countries (Denmark, Norway, Sweden and Finland) have enacted a revised Nordic Maritime Code with effect from 1 October 1994. Whilst the Scandinavian countries maintain that they remain signatories to and appliers of the Hague-Visby Rules, their leaning towards Hamburg has long been known and this new Code makes it even more obvious.

Whether the Code conflicts with the Hague-Visby Rules is debatable. Certainly it has seized upon every point where Hague-Visby allowed freedom of contract and removed that freedom with a Hamburg solution. In this it clearly adopts the UNCTAD/ICC Rules approach and the influence of the chairman of the committee that drafted those Rules (Professor J. Ramberg of Stockholm University) is obvious.

Amongst the Hamburg points in the Nordic Code are the following:

1. *Period of Cover*: receipt to delivery instead of loading to discharge.
2. *Applicable to all contracts of carriage by sea, except Charter Parties*: not restricted to bills of lading.
3. *Carrier is liable for delay up to $2\frac{1}{2} \times freight$*: no such provision in Hague-Visby.
4. *Live animals and deck cargo are covered by the Rules*: freedom of contract in Hague-Visby.
5. *The "menu" approach of Hague-Visby Article IV, Rule 2* is rejected in favour of one that looks rather like the UNCTAD/ICC Rules approach, which in turn bears striking resemblance to Hamburg Rules Article 5, Rule 1 with Fire and Nautical Fault added back. Professor Ramberg claims that this approach is not a departure from Hague-Visby Article IV, Rule 2. If I attended the Inns of Court and asked for volunteers to contest this statement I would expect to be trampled in the stampede ensuing!

Even if the Scandinavians are Hague-Visby in word they clearly are not in spirit and lean heavily towards Hamburg and UNCTAD/ICC Rules, under the considerable influence of their academics.

USA

The greatest challenge to the uniformity of approach internationally to rules governing the liability of carriers for the carriage of goods by sea comes from the nation most likely to influence others to follow. Whilst the departure from the uniform approach is unfortunate, at least the US approach is reasonable, logical and constructive.

It started, rather like the Australian model, from an attempt to identify and resolve the differences between the carrier and cargo interests' requirements and, in this case, the review was conducted by the US Maritime Law Association (MLA), who (at the time) were assured that, if they could secure agreement between the parties interested. Congressional time would be made available for revising the '36 COGSA. Agreement was reached at the MLA Meeting in May 1996 and the revised draft presently awaits enactment. Whilst there are no guarantees, those most closely involved expect enactment during the present Congress, probably some time in 1998.

Significant changes during the legislative process are not anticipated but, of course, anything can happen. However, the US development is important enough and likely to be substantially influential, that it is worthwhile commenting on the MLA draft presently before Congress to repeal the US COGSA 1936 (*see* Appendix VI). (The Draft is reproduced by kind permission of Professor Michael F. Sturley, Rosenberg Centennial Professor of Law at the University of Texas at Austin, who was Reporter to the MLA Committee that prepared the Draft and upon whose extensive explanatory notes: Proposed Amendments to the Carriage of Goods By Sea Act, published in the Houston Journal of International Law 609 (1996), I have drawn in preparing this commentary.) (Anyone seeking a greater in depth study of the Draft should obtain this publication which provides an insider's perspective of the development of the Draft.)

As even a cursory glance at the Proposed Bill quickly reveals, whilst much of its content may be based upon the Hague-Visby Rules, the drafting of the Bill follows that of the Rules hardly at all. The MLA has a ready and valid excuse for this, which is that a plethora of US case law on the 1936 COGSA has led the American interpretation of the rules substantially away from the general international understanding, so that positive action is necessary to bring US law on this subject back into line with that elsewhere. This certainly covers a substantive part of the "non-Hague-Visby drafting" but one has to observe that "having got the bit between the teeth", the MLA has taken the opportunity to update the Hague-Visby Rules to cover developments since they were drafted, particularly in the field of multimodal transport. What influence this will have on the development of this subject internationally remains to be seen.

The Proposed Bill is quite a lengthy document upon which to comment so the following observations are merely intended to draw attention to the main points and changes, identifying their location for more detailed study.

Period of application [1301(e) & 1302] [p. 136]

Instead of the traditional Hague Rules "tackle-to-tackle" period or even the Hamburg Rules "receipt at the port to delivery at the port" the Proposed Bill goes the whole hog and applies to multimodal contracts throughout, including the land carriage. It applies to contracting carriers throughout and to performing carriers, except road and rail carriers, where multimodal contracts of carriage, which include ocean transit, are involved. The Act is only mandatorily applied to foreign trade but has the force of law in domestic trade if contractually incorporated. Unimodal contracts for Great Lakes, rivers or other inland waters, or the intercoastal waterway are also excluded [1301(b)].

Scope of application [1301(b) & (g) & 1303(4)(b)(1)] [p. 136 and p. 139]

The Act applies to all contracts of carriage, other than charterparties, "for the carriage of goods either by sea or partially by sea and partially by one or more other modes of transportation". Accordingly the Act specifically applies to Waybills and Electronic Bills of Lading (if and when they materialise).

Deck cargo and live animals [1301(c)] [p. 136]

The Hague-Visby Rules allows freedom of contract for these cargoes. The Act applies to deck cargo but not to live animals.

The navigational fault exception [1304(2) proviso] [p. 146]

In its first meeting in April 1992 the "Ad Hoc Liability Rules Study Group" of the MLA quickly established that there was no chance of proceeding towards any type of agreement on a draft which contained the nautical fault exception (Article IV, Rule 2(a) of the Hague and Hague-Visby Rules). Cargo interests saw this as a bizarre situation where a contractor escapes liability by proving that he has been negligent and were determined that this approach should not be retained. To carriers it represented an equitable risk sharing arrangement, where large sums of money were at risk in a mutual adventure, where the carrier was substantially exposed in the shape of his ship and thus provided with adequate incentive to care.

The compromise (if you can call it that) was to delete the exclusion but to put the onus of proof on the claimant to prove negligence by the carrier in order to succeed in a case involving negligent navigation or management of the ship.

Another addition to the Hague/Hague-Visby "menu" is the provision that, if a loss or damage is partially caused by an excluded peril and one for which the carrier is liable, the carrier is liable to the extent that the factor for which he is liable caused the loss or damage and, if there is insufficient evidence to show what percentage of blame is attributable to the carrier he shall bear 50 per cent of the claim for loss or damage.

The fire exception [1304(2)(b)] [p. 145]

Whilst the general scope of the protection of the Rules is widened in the Act (*see* below) the benefit of the fire exclusion is reserved to the ocean carrier and the contracting carrier, both of whose protection is negated in the event of actual fault or privity.

Limitation of liability [1304(5)] [p. 147]

This was another area where cargo interests demanded a change and the Hague-Visby Rules SDR Protocol approach was adopted with the weight and package alternative.

Service contracts [1303(8)(a)] [p. 145]

Whereas the Hague and Hague-Visby Rules are mandatory for all consignments where a Bill of Lading is issued the Act allows Service Contracts to vary liabilities between the signatory parties to limits below those in the Act.

"Unbreakable limitation" [1304(4) & (5)(e)] [p. 147 and p. 148]

The Hague-Visby Article IV, Rule 5(e) approach is adopted here with a note to the effect that the right to limit is lost only by the carrier guilty of breach and the other carriers can continue to enjoy this protection.

This provision is a great improvement for the carrier who is denied the opportunity to limit liability in US courts under '36 COGSA (as interpreted by case law) almost literally at the drop of a hat. It defeats the doctrine of fundamental breach which, in US courts, had viewed the slightest thing as a fundamental breach worthy of denying the carrier the protection of the contract and the '36 Act. Trivia like:

- shipment on deck without shipper's permission or claused B/L (*Encyclopaedia Britannica Inc.* v. *"Hong Kong Producer"* 422 F2d 7 (2nd Cir 1969));
- failure to give the shipper "a fair opportunity" to declare a higher value and receive an Ad Valorem Bill of Lading (*Pan Am World Airways* v. *California Stevedore & Ballast Co.* 559 F2d 1173 (9th Cir 1977));

are all swept away to create a much more reasonable environment for the carrier. In 1304(4) it is specifically provided that geographical deviation is not a fundamental breach of contract and the carrier can still claim the benefit of the Act's protections. (*See* comment on Hague-Visby Rules Article IV, Rule 4 (page 40) and compare with US approach.)

The "Himalaya" problem [1301(a)(iii)] [p. 136]

How effectively to give servants, agents and sub-contractors the benefit of the contract of carriage has exercised the minds of carriers since Mrs Adler succeeded in circumventing the terms of her passage ticket on the P & O vessel "Himalaya" (*see* page 50). Article IV *bis*, Rule 2 of the Hague-Visby Rules protects servants and agents but not independent sub-contractors so the comprehensive protection encompassed in the Act is welcome to carriers. It is achieved within the definition of "performing carrier" in (a)(iii) which automatically brings the party concerned within the definition of carrier in (a)(i).

Protection against tortious actions [1300] [p. 135]

Lawyers frequently seek to circumvent inconvenient provisions in any Act by bringing their actions in tort. Protection for carriers against this tactic is provided in the preamble of the Act where it is provided that . . . "the Act shall constitute the complete and exclusive remedy against the carrier" . . . (Hague-Visby Article IV *bis*, Rule 1).

Jurisdiction [1303(8)(b)] [p. 145]

Following a nasty shock in the "Sky Reefer" (*Vimar Seguros Y Reaseguros S.A. v. Sky Reefer* 29 F3d 727 1994 AMC 2513 (1st Cir. 1994)), in which a foreign arbitration clause was recognised and given effect, New York lawyers have moved with understandable despatch to close this potential escape route for their potential business! Foreign jurisdiction and arbitration clauses are out-lawed!

Qualifying statements [1303(3)] [p. 137]

The Act recognises the changes brought about by containerisation and provides to cover them in some detail. After providing for the carrier to issue a negotiable bill of lading or a non-negotiable bill of lading (or other non-negotiable document) upon the demand of the shipper and containing at least the stated minimum data (Hague-Visby Rules, Article III, Rules 3, 4, 5 & 7), the Act provides for:

- clausing FCL bills of lading "said to contain";
- carrier not liable for shortages if container delivered seal intact;
- carrier needs to clause bill to effect that container not weighed if liability is to be avoided for deficient weight.

Pomerene Act [1303(4)] [p. 139]

This subsection of the Act incorporates 16 amended sections of the original Pomerene Act (Federal Bill of Lading Act 1916 (as subsequently amended)), which remains in full force and is not repealed by implication so that it can continue to apply to domestic shipments. As the Act applies to imports and exports the revised Pomerene provisions in the Act, which governs international trade only, are applicable to imports as well as exports, whereas the Pomerene Act applies only to exports and inter-state traffic. This change has important implications where straight bills of lading (i.e. not made out to order and non-negotiable) are concerned.

Where there are inconsistencies between the Pomerene Act and the new COGSA Act the latter prevails but otherwise they run in parallel.

Conclusion

The changes, as can be seen from the comments above, are quite radical and were opposed by the International Chamber of Shipping, the International Pool Group of P & I Clubs and the Baltic and International Maritime Council (BIMCO), who oppose departure from the Hague/Hague-Visby approach on the grounds that this defeats the goal of international uniformity. These objections are unlikely to carry much weight with the US and could just have the opposite effect in stiffening their resolve to "do their own thing" (they have a long history of taking this view) and not allowing themselves to be dictated to by the rest of the world.

PART 4

CMI UNIFORM RULES FOR SEA WAYBILLS AND CMI RULES FOR ELECTRONIC BILLS OF LADING

At their 1990 Conference in Paris the Comité Maritime International approved the above two sets of Rules which were designed to promote the use of Waybills and Electronic Bills of Lading.

CMI UNIFORM RULES FOR SEA WAYBILLS

These admirably brief set of rules provide as follows:

1. Scope of application

    (i) These Rules shall be called the "CMI Uniform Rules for Sea Waybills".

    (ii) They shall apply when adopted by a contract of carriage which is not covered by a bill of lading or similar document of title, whether the contract be in writing or not.

2. Definitions

In these Rules:

    "Contract of carriage" shall mean any contract of carriage subject to these Rules which is to be performed wholly or partly by sea.

    "Goods" shall mean any goods carried or received for carriage under a contract of carriage.

    "Carrier" and "Shipper" shall mean the parties named in or identifiable as such from the contract of carriage.

    "Consignee" shall mean the party named in or identifiable as such from the contract of carriage, or any person substituted as consignee in accordance with rule 6(i).

    "Right of Control" shall mean the rights and obligations referred to in rule 6.

3. Agency*

(i) The shipper on entering into the contract of carriage does so not only on his own behalf but also as agent for and on behalf of the consignee, and warrants to the carrier that he has authority so to do.

(ii) This rule shall apply if, and only if, it be necessary by the law applicable to the contract of carriage so as to enable the consignee to sue and be sued thereon. The consignee shall be under no greater liability that he would have been had the contract of carriage been covered by a bill of lading or similar document of title.

4. Rights and responsibilities

(i) The contract of carriage shall be subject to any International Convention or National Law which is, or if the contract of carriage had been covered by a Bill of Lading or similar document of title would have been, compulsorily applicable thereto. Such convention or law shall apply notwithstanding anything inconsistent therewith in the contract of carriage.

(ii) Subject always to subrule (i), the contract of carriage is governed by:
   (a) these Rules;
   (b) unless otherwise agreed by the parties, the carrier's standard terms and conditions for the trade, if any, including any terms and conditions relating to the non-sea part of the carriage;
   (c) any other terms and conditions agreed by the parties

(iii) In the event of any inconsistency between the terms and conditions mentioned under subrule (ii)(b) or (c) and these Rules, these Rules shall prevail.

5. Description of the goods

(i) The shipper warrants the accuracy of the particulars furnished by him relating to the goods, and shall indemnify the carrier against any loss, damage or expense resulting from any inaccuracy.

(ii) In the absence of reservation by the carrier, any statement in a sea waybill or similar document as to the quantity or condition of the goods shall
   (a) as between the carrier and the shipper be *prima facie* evidence of receipt of the goods as so stated;
   (b) as between the carrier and the consignee be conclusive evidence of receipt of the goods as so stated, and proof to the contrary

* Enactment of the Carriage of Goods by Sea Act 1992 in the United Kingdom rendered this provision superfluous under Engish law.

shall not be permitted, provided always that the consignee has acted in good faith.

6. Right of control

(i) Unless the shipper has exercised his option under sub-rule (ii) below, he shall be the only party entitled to give the carrier instructions in relation to the contract of carriage. Unless prohibited by the applicable law, he shall be entitled to change the name of the consignee at any time up to the consignee claiming delivery of the goods after their arrival at destination, provided he gives the carrier reasonable notice in writing, or by some other means acceptable to the carrier, thereby undertaking to indemnify the carrier against any additional expense caused thereby.

(ii) The shipper shall have the option, to be exercised not later than the receipt of the goods by the carrier, to transfer the right of control to the consignee. The exercise of this option must be noted on the sea waybill or similar document, if any. Where the option has been exercised the consignee shall have such rights as are referred to in subrule (i) above and the shipper shall cease to have such rights.

7. Delivery

(i) The carrier shall deliver the goods to the consignee upon production of proper identification.

(ii) The carrier shall be under no liability for wrong delivery if he can prove that he has exercised reasonable care to ascertain that the party claiming to be the consignee is in fact that party.

8. Validity

In the event of anything contained in these Rules or any such provisions as are incorporated into the contract of carriage by virtue of rule 4, being inconsistent with the provisions of any International Convention or National law compulsorily applicable to the contract of carriage, such rules and provisions shall to that extent but no further be null and void.

The Rules need to be contractually incorporated into waybills (or other non-negotiable transport documents) and, whilst the title refers to sea waybills to differentiate from air waybills, combined transport (or multimodal) waybills can apply these Rules (*see* definition of Contract of Carriage).

As the waybill is not a transferable contract, like a bill of lading, Rule 3 is provided for those countries where it is necessary to bind the consignee into the contract, initially entered into between the shipper and the carrier.

Rule 4 ensures that the recourse under a waybill is at least as good as under a bill of lading by applying any law which would be mandatory if the waybill were a bill of lading and the same conditions that would apply if the carrier issued a bill of lading. So, if a waybill is issued "Subject to the CMI Uniform Rules for Sea Waybills", as evidenced by words to this effect thereon, the merchant is guaranteed recourse terms at least as good as if he held a bill of lading.

Rule 6 sets out the rights of the shipper to stoppage in transit and, how he can surrender these rights in favour of the consignee.

Rule 7 provides for delivery against proof of identity rather than surrender of a document.

Along with the rights conferred on a consignee in the Carriage of Goods by Sea Act 1992, the Uniform Rules for Sea Waybills make waybills a more attractive proposition than bills of lading in certain circumstances.

CMI RULES FOR ELECTRONIC BILLS OF LADING

These Rules are rather more extensive and, since their "birth" at the 1990 CMI Conference, much time effort and money has been expended by several parties trying to produce a workable scheme based upon the Rules, which provide as follows:

1. Scope of application

These rules shall apply whenever the parties so agree.

2. Definitions

    (a)   "Contract of Carriage" means any agreement to carry goods wholly or partly by sea.

    (b)   "EDI" means Electronic Data Interchange, i.e. the interchange of trade data effected by teletransmission.

    (c)   "UN/EDIFACT" means the United Nations Rules for Electronic Data Interchange for Administration, Commerce and Transport.

    (d)   "Transmission" means one or more message electronically sent together as one unit of despatch which includes heading and terminating data.

    (e)   "Confirmation" means a Transmission which advises that the content of a Transmission appears to be complete and correct, without prejudice to any subsequent consideration or action that the content may warrant.

    (f)   "Private Key" means any technically appropriate form, such as a combination of numbers and/or letters which the parties may agree for securing the authenticity and integrity of a Transmission.

(g) "Holder" means the party who is entitled to the rights described in Article 7(a) by virtue of its possession of a valid Private Key.

(h) "Electronic Monitoring System" means the device by which a computer system can be examined for the transactions that it recorded, such as a Trade Data Log or an Audit Trail.

(i) "Electronic Storage" means any temporary, intermediate or permanent storage of electronic data including the primary and the back up storage of such data.

3. Rules of procedure

(a) When not in conflict with these Rules, the Uniform Rules of Conduct for Interchange of Trade Data by Teletransmission, 1987 (UNCID) shall govern the conduct between the parties.

(b) The EDI under these Rules should conform with the relevant UN/EDIFACT standards. However, the parties may use any other method of trade data interchange acceptable to all of the users.

(c) Unless otherwise agreed, the document format for the Contract of Carriage shall conform to the UN Layout Key or compatible national standard for bills of lading.

(d) Unless otherwise agreed, a recipient of a Transmission is not authorised to act on a Transmission unless he has sent a Confirmation.

(e) In the event of a dispute arising between the parties as to the data actually transmitted, an Electronic Monitoring System may be used to verify the data received. Data concerning other transactions not related to the data in dispute are to be considered as trade secrets and thus not available for examination. If such data are unavoidably revealed as part of the examination of the Electronic Monitoring System, they must be treated as confidential and not released to any outside party or used for any other purpose.

(f) Any transfer of rights to the goods shall be considered to be private information and shall not be released to any outside party not connected to the transport or clearance of the goods.

4. Form and content of the receipt message

(a) The carrier, upon receiving the goods from the shipper, shall give notice of the receipt of the goods to the shipper by a message at the electronic address specified by the shipper.

(b) This receipt message shall include:
   (i) the name of the shipper;
   (ii) the description of the goods, with any representations and reservations in the same tenor as would be required if a paper bill of lading were issued;
   (iii) the date and place of the receipt of the goods;

       (iv) a reference to the carrier's terms and conditions of carriage;
        and

       (v) the Private Key to be used in subsequent Transmissions.

      The shipper must confirm this receipt message to the carrier, upon
      which confirmation the shipper shall be the Holder.

(c) Upon demand of the Holder, the receipt message shall be updated
      with the date and place of shipment as soon as the goods have been
      loaded on board.

(d) The information contained in (ii), (iii) and (iv) of paragraph (b)
      above including the date and place of shipment if updated in accor-
      dance with paragraph (c) of this Rule, shall have the same force and
      effect as if the receipt message were contained in a paper bill of
      lading.

5. Terms and conditions of the contract of carriage

(a) It is agreed and understood that whenever the carrier makes a refer-
      ence to its terms and conditions of carriage, these terms and condi-
      tions shall form part of the Contract of Carriage.

(b) Such terms and conditions must be readily available to the parties to
      the Contract of Carriage.

(c) In the event of any conflict or inconsistency between such terms and
      conditions and these Rules, these Rules shall prevail.

6. Applicable law

The Contract of Carriage shall be subject to any international convention or
national law which would have been compulsorily applicable if a paper bill of
lading had been issued.

7. Right of control and transfer

(a) The Holder is the only party who may, as against the carrier:

      (1) claim delivery of the goods;

      (2) nominate the consignee or substitute a nominated consignee for
         any other party, including itself;

      (3) transfer the Right of Control and Transfer to another party;

      (4) instruct the carrier on any other subject concerning the goods in
         accordance with the terms and conditions of the Contract of
         Carriage as if he were the holder of a paper bill of lading.

(b) A transfer of the Right of Control and Transfer shall be effected;

      (i) by notification of the current Holder to the carrier of its inten-
        tion to transfer its Right of Control and Transfer to a proposed
        new Holder, and

(ii) confirmation by the carrier of such notification message, whereupon

(iii) the carrier shall transmit the information as referred to in Article 4 (except for the Private Key) to the proposed new Holder, whereafter

(iv) the proposed new Holder shall advise the carrier of its acceptance of the Right of Control and Transfer, whereupon

(v) the carrier shall cancel the current Private Key and issue a new Private Key to the new Holder.

(c) If the proposed new Holder advises the carrier that it does not accept the Right of Control and Transfer or fails to advise the carrier of such acceptance within a reasonable time, the proposed transfer of the Right of Control and Transfer shall not take place. The carrier shall notify the current Holder accordingly and the current Private Key shall retain its validity.

(d) The transfer of the Right of Control and Transfer in the manner described above shall have the same effect as the transfer of such rights under a paper Bill of Lading.

8. The Private Key

(a) The Private Key is unique to each successive Holder. It is not transferable by the Holder. The carrier and the Holder shall each maintain the security of the Private Key.

(b) The carrier shall only be obliged to send a Confirmation of an electronic message to the last Holder to whom it issued a Private Key when such Holder secures the Transmission containing such electronic message by the use of the Private Key.

(c) The Private Key must be separate and distinct from any means used to identify the Contract of Carriage and any security password or identification used to access the computer network.

9. Delivery

(a) The carrier shall notify the Holder of the place and date of intended delivery of the goods. Upon such notification the Holder has a duty to nominate a consignee and to give adequate delivery instructions to the carrier with verification by the Private Key. In the absence of such nomination, the Holder will be deemed to be the consignee.

(b) The carrier shall deliver the goods to the consignee upon production of proper identification in accordance with the delivery instructions specified in paragraph (a) above; such delivery shall automatically cancel the Private Key.

(c)   The carrier shall be under no liability for misdelivery if it can prove that it exercised reasonable care to ascertain that the party who claimed to be the consignee was in fact that party.

10. Option to receive a paper document

(a)   The Holder has the option at any time prior to delivery of the goods to demand from the carrier a paper bill of lading. Such document shall be made available at a location to be determined by the Holder, provided that no carrier shall be obliged to make such document available at a place where it has no facilities and in such instance the carrier shall only be obliged to make the document available at the facility nearest to the location determined by the Holder. The carrier shall not be responsible for delays in delivering the goods resulting from the Holder exercising the above option.

(b)   The carrier has the option at any time prior to delivery of the goods to issue to the Holder a paper bill of lading unless the exercise of such option could result in undue delay or disrupts the delivery of the goods.

(c)   A bill of lading issued under Rules 10(a) or (b) shall include:
   (i)   the information set out in the receipt message referred to in Rule 4 (except for the Private Key); and
   (ii) a statement to the effect that the bill of lading has been issued upon termination of the procedures for EDI under the CMI Rules for Electronic Bills of Lading. The aforementioned bill of lading shall be issued at the option of the Holder either to the order of the Holder whose name for this purpose shall then be inserted in the bill of lading or "to bearer".

(d)   The issuance of a paper bill of lading under Rule 10(a) or (b) shall cancel the Private Key and terminate the procedures for EDI under these Rules. Termination of these procedures by the Holder or the carrier will not relieve any of the parties to the Contract of Carriage or their rights, obligations or liabilities while performing under the present Rules nor of their rights, obligations or liabilities under the Contract of Carriage.

(e)   The Holder may demand at any time the issuance of a print-out of the receipt message referred to in Rule 4 (except for the Private key) marked as "non-negotiable copy". The issuance of such a print-out shall not cancel the Private Key nor terminate the procedures for EDI.

11. Electronic data is equivalent to writing

The carrier and the shipper and all subsequent parties utilizing these procedures agree that any national or local law, custom or practice requiring the Contract of Carriage to be evidenced in writing and signed, is satisfied by the transmitted and confirmed electronic data residing on computer data storage media displayable in human language on a video screen or as printed out by a computer. In agreeing to adopt these Rules, the parties shall be taken to have agreed not to raise the defence that this contract is not in writing.

A project known as "Bolero", which is presently sponsored by the inter-bank settlement organisation, SWIFT and the combined transport operators mutual insurer, The TT Club, seeks to apply the concept of these Rules via a Central Operating Unit (to be run by SWIFT) to create a system to facilitate "paperless trading". A "Club", The Bolero Association, has been formed and to engage in paperless trading it will be necessary to be a member of the Club (with subscriptions fully paid).

The idea is sound but there are practical operational, legal and other problems to be overcome before the project can proceed. It is hoped to run a pilot scheme later in 1998. It remains to be seen if this will provide the means of transferring from paper-based to paperless trading or whether some less sophisticated and expensive alternative can be found. A system utilising waybills has been suggested as a possible alternative. Only time will tell whether Bolero succeeds.

HAGUE & HAGUE-VISBY RULES

HAGUE RULES—UNITED KINGDOM CARRIAGE OF GOODS BY SEA ACT 1924

An Act to amend the law with respect to the carriage of goods by sea. (1st August, 1924.)

WHEREAS at the International Conference on Maritime Law held at Brussels in October, 1922, the delegates at the Conference, including the delegates representing His Majesty, agreed unanimously to recommend their respective Governments to adopt as the basis of a convention a draft convention for the unification of certain rules relating to bills of lading:

And whereas at a meeting held at Brussels in October, 1923, the rules contained in the said draft convention were amended by the Committee appointed by the said Conference:

And whereas it is expedient that the said rules as so amended and as set out with modifications in the Schedule to this Act (in this Act referred to as "the Rules") should, subject to the provisions of this Act, be given the force of law with a view to establishing the responsibilities, liabilities, rights and immunities attaching to carriers under bills of lading:

Be it therefore enacted by the King's most Excellent Majesty, by and with the advice and consent of the Lords Spiritual and Temporal, and Commons, in this present Parliament assembled, and by the authority of the same, as follows:—

Application of Rules in Schedule [p. 2]

1. Subject to the provisions of this Act, the Rules shall have effect in relation to and in connection with the carriage of goods by sea in ships carrying goods from any port in Great Britain or Northern Ireland to any other port whether in or outside Great Britain or Northern Ireland.

Absolute warranty of seaworthiness not to be implied in contracts to which Rules apply [p. 3]

2. There shall not be implied in any contract for the carriage of goods by sea to which the Rules apply any absolute undertaking by the carrier of the goods to provide a seaworthy ship.

Statement as to application of Rules to be included in bills of lading [p. 3]

3. Every bill of lading, or similar document of title, issued in Great Britain or Northern Ireland which contains or is evidence of any contract to which the Rules apply shall contain an express statement that it is to have effect subject to the provisions of the said Rules as applied by this Act.

Modification of Article VI of Rules in relation to coasting trade [p. 2]

4. Article VI of the Rules shall, in relation to the carriage of goods by sea in ships carrying goods from any port in Great Britain or Northern Ireland to any other port in Great Britain or Northern Ireland or to a port in the Irish Free State, have effect as though the said Article referred to goods of any class instead of to particular goods and as though the proviso to the second paragraph of the said Article were omitted.

Modification of Rules 4 and 5 of Article III in relation to bulk cargoes [p. 3]

5. Where under the custom of any trade the weight of any bulk cargo inserted in the bill of lading is a weight ascertained or accepted by a third party other than the carrier or the shipper and the fact that the weight is so ascertained or accepted is stated in the bill of lading, then, notwithstanding anything in the Rules, the bill of lading shall not be deemed to be *prima facie* evidence against the carrier of the receipt of goods of the weight so inserted in the bill of lading, and the accuracy thereof at the time of shipment shall not be deemed to have been guaranteed by the shipper.

Short title, saving and operation [p. 4]

6.—(1) This Act may be cited as the Carriage of Goods by Sea Act, 1924.

(2) Nothing in this Act shall affect the operation of sections four hundred and forty-six to four hundred and fifty, both inclusive, five hundred and two, and five hundred and three of the Merchant Shipping Act, 1894, as amended by any subsequent enactment, or the operation of any other enactment for the time being in force limiting the liability of the owners of seagoing vessels.

(3) The Rules shall not by virtue of this Act apply to any contract for the carriage of goods by sea made before such day, not being earlier than the thirtieth day of June, nineteen hundred and twenty-four, as His Majesty may by Order in Council direct, nor to any bill of lading or similar document of

title issued, whether before or after such day as aforesaid, in pursuance of any such contract as aforesaid.

SCHEDULE. RULES RELATING TO BILLS OF LADING

Article I. Definitions [p. 15]

In these Rules the following expressions have the meanings hereby assigned to them respectively, that is to say—

- (a) "Carrier" includes the owner or the charterer who enters into a contract of carriage with a shipper:
- (b) "Contract of carriage" applies only to contracts of carriage covered by a bill of lading or any similar document of title, in so far as such document relates to the carriage of goods by sea, including any bill of lading or any similar document as aforesaid issued under or pursuant to a charterparty from the moment at which such bill of lading or similar document of title regulates the relations between a carrier and a holder of the same:—
- (c) "Goods" includes goods, wares, merchandises, and articles of every kind whatsoever, except live animals and cargo which by the contract of carriage is stated as being carried on deck and is so carried:
- (d) "Ship" means any vessel used for the carriage of goods by sea:
- (e) "Carriage of goods" covers the period from the time when the goods are loaded on to the time when they are discharged from the ship.

Article II. Risks [p. 19]

Subject to the provisions of Article VI, under every contract of carriage of goods by sea the carrier, in relation to the loading, handling, stowage, carriage, custody, care, and discharge of such goods, shall be subject to the responsibilities and liabilities, and entitled to the rights and immunities hereinafter set forth.

Article III. Responsibilities and liabilities [p. 19]

1. The carrier shall be bound, before and at the beginning of the voyage, to exercise due diligence to—

- (a) Make the ship seaworthy:
- (b) Properly man, equip, and supply the ship:
- (c) Make the holds, refrigerating and cool chambers, and all other parts of the ship in which goods are carried, fit and safe for their reception, carriage and preservation.

2. Subject to the provisions of Article IV, the carrier shall properly and carefully load, handle, stow, carry, keep, care for and discharge the goods carried.

3. After receiving the goods into his charge, the carrier, or the master or agent of the carrier, shall, on demand of the shipper, issue to the shipper a bill of lading showing among other things—

(a) The leading marks necessary for identification of the goods as the same are furnished in writing by the shipper before the loading of such goods starts, provided such marks are stamped or otherwise shown clearly upon the goods if uncovered, or on the cases or coverings in which such goods are contained, in such a manner as should ordinarily remain legible until the end of the voyage;

(b) Either the number of packages or pieces, or the quantity, or weight, as the case may be, as furnished in writing by the shipper;

(c) The apparent order and condition of the goods:

Provided that no carrier, master or agent of the carrier, shall be bound to state or show in the bill of lading any marks, number, quantity, or weight which he has reasonable ground for suspecting not accurately to represent the goods actually received, or which he has had no reasonable means of checking.

4. Such a bill of lading shall be *prima facie* evidence of the receipt by the carrier of the goods as therein described in accordance with paragraph 3(*a*), (*b*), and (*c*).

5. The shipper shall be deemed to have guaranteed to the carrier the accuracy at the time of shipment of the marks, number, quantity, and weight, as furnished by him, and the shipper shall indemnify the carrier against all loss, damages, and expenses arising or resulting from inaccuracies in such particulars. The right of the carrier to such indemnity shall in no way limit his responsibility and liability under the contract of carriage to any person other than the shipper.

6. Unless notice of loss or damage and the general nature of such loss or damage be given in writing to the carrier or his agent at the port of discharge before or at the time of the removal of the goods into the custody of the person entitled to delivery thereof under the contract of carriage, or, if the loss or damage be not apparent, within three days, such removal shall be *prima facie* evidence of the delivery by the carrier of the goods as described in the bill of lading.

The notice in writing need not be given if the state of the goods has at the time of their receipt been the subject of joint survey or inspection.

In any event the carrier and the ship shall be discharged from all liability in respect of loss or damage unless suit is brought within one year after delivery of the goods or the date when the goods should have been delivered.

In the case of any actual or apprehended loss or damage the carrier and the receiver shall give all reasonable facilities to each other for inspecting and tallying the goods.

7. After the goods are loaded the bill of lading to be issued by the carrier, master or agent of the carrier, to the shipper shall, if the shipper so demands, be a "shipped" bill of lading, provided that if the shipper shall have previously taken up any document of title to such goods, he shall surrender the same as against the issue of the "shipped" bill of lading, but at the option of the carrier such document of title may be noted at the port of shipment by the carrier, master, or agent with the name or names of the ship or ships upon which the goods have been shipped and the date or dates of shipment, and when so noted the same shall for the purpose of this Article be deemed to constitute a "shipped" bill of lading.

8. Any clause, covenant or agreement in a contract of carriage relieving the carrier or the ship from liability for loss or damage to or in connection with goods arising from negligence, fault or failure in the duties and obligations provided in this Article or lessening such liability otherwise than as provided in these Rules, shall be null and void and of no effect.

A benefit of insurance or similar clause shall be deemed to be a clause relieving the carrier from liability.

Article IV. Rights and immunities [p. 31]

1. Neither the carrier nor the ship shall be liable for loss or damage arising or resulting from unseaworthiness unless caused by want of due diligence on the part of the carrier to make the ship seaworthy, and to secure that the ship is properly manned, equipped and supplied, and to make the holds, refrigerating and cool chambers and all other parts of the ship in which goods are carried fit and safe for their reception, carriage and preservation in accordance with the provisions of paragraph 1 of Article III. Whenever loss or damage has resulted from unseaworthiness, the burden of proving the exercise of due diligence shall be on the carrier or other person claiming exemption under this section.

2. Neither the carrier nor the ship shall be responsible for loss or damage arising or resulting from—

    (a) Act, neglect, or default of the master, mariner, pilot, or the servants of the carrier in the navigation or in the management of the ship:

    (b) Fire, unless caused by the actual fault or privity of the carrier:

    (c) Perils, dangers and accidents of the sea or other navigable waters:

    (d) Act of God:

    (e) Act of war:

    (f) Act of public enemies:

    (g) Arrest or restraint of princes, rulers or people, or seizure under legal process:

    (h) Quarantine restrictions:

    (i) Act or omission of the shipper or owner of the goods, his agent or representative:

(*j*)   Strikes or lock-outs or stoppage or restrain of labour from whatever cause, whether partial or general:

(*k*)   Riots and civil commotions:

(*l*)   Saving or attempting to save life or property at sea:

(*m*)   Wastage in bulk or weight or any other loss or damage arising from inherent defect, quality, or vice of the goods:

(*n*)   Insufficiency of packing:

(*o*)   Insufficiency or inadequacy of marks:

(*p*)   Latent defects not discoverable by due diligence:

(*q*)   Any other cause arising without the actual fault or privity of the carrier, or without the fault or neglect of the agents or servants of the carrier, but the burden of proof shall be on the person claiming the benefit of this exception to show that neither the actual fault or privity of the carrier nor the fault or neglect of the agents or servants of the carrier contributed to the loss or damage.

3. The shipper shall not be responsible for loss or damage sustained by the carrier or the ship arising or resulting from any cause without the act, fault or neglect of the shipper, his agents or his servants.

4. Any deviation in saving or attempting to save life or property at sea, or any reasonable deviation shall not be deemed to be an infringement or breach of these Rules or of the contract of carriage, and the carrier shall not be liable for any loss or damage resulting therefrom.

5. Neither the carrier nor the ship shall in any event be or become liable for any loss or damage to or in connection with goods in an amount exceeding 100*l.* per package or unit, or the equivalent of that sum in other currency, unless the nature and value of such goods have been declared by the shipper before shipment and inserted in the bill of lading.

This declaration if embodied in the bill of lading shall be *prima facie* evidence, but shall not be binding or conclusive on the carrier.

By agreement between the carrier, master or agent of the carrier and the shipper another maximum amount than that mentioned in this paragraph may be fixed, provided that such maximum shall not be less than the figure above named.

Neither the carrier nor the ship shall be responsible in any event for loss or damage to or in connection with goods if the nature or value thereof has been knowingly misstated by the shipper in the bill of lading.

6. Goods of an inflammable, explosive or dangerous nature to the shipment whereof the carrier, master or agent of the carrier, has not consented, with knowledge of their nature and character, may at any time before discharge be landed at any place or destroyed or rendered innocuous by the carrier without compensation, and the shipper of such goods shall be liable for all damages and expenses directly or indirectly arising out of or resulting from such shipment.

If any such goods shipped with such knowledge and consent shall become a danger to the ship or cargo, they may in like manner be landed at any place or destroyed or rendered innocuous by the carrier without liability on the part of the carrier except to general average, if any.

Article V. Surrender of rights and immunities, and increase of responsibilities and liabilities [p. 51]

A carrier shall be at liberty to surrender in whole or in part all or any of his rights and immunities or to increase any of his responsibilities or liabilities under the Rules contained in any of these Articles, provided such surrender or increase shall be embodied in the bill or lading issued to the shipper.

The provisions of these Rules shall not be applicable to charterparties, but if bills of lading are issued in the case of a ship under a charterparty they shall comply with the terms of these Rules. Nothing in these Rules shall be held to prevent the insertion in a bill of lading of any lawful provision regarding general average.

Article VI. Special conditions [p. 52]

Notwithstanding the provisions of the preceding Articles, a carrier, master or agent of the carrier, and a shipper shall in regard to any particular goods be at liberty to enter into any agreement in any terms as to the responsibility and liability of the carrier for such goods, and as to the rights and immunities of the carrier in respect of such goods, or his obligation as to seaworthiness, so far as this stipulation is not contrary to public policy, or the care or diligence of his servants or agents in regard to the loading, handling, stowage, carriage, custody, care, and discharge of the goods carried by sea, provided that in this case no bill of lading has been or shall be issued and that the terms agreed shall be embodied in a receipt which shall be a non-negotiable document and shall be marked as such.

Any agreement so entered into shall have full legal effect:

Provided that this Article shall not apply to ordinary commercial shipments made in the ordinary course of trade, but only to other shipments where the character or condition of the property to be carried or the circumstances, terms and conditions under which the carriage is to be performed, are such as reasonably to justify a special agreement.

Article VII. Limitations on the application of the Rules [p. 53]

Nothing herein contained shall prevent a carrier or a shipper from entering into any agreement, stipulation, condition, reservation or exemption as to the responsibility and liability of the carrier or the ship for the loss or damage to or in connection with the custody and care and handling of goods prior to the loading on and subsequent to the discharge from the ship on which the goods are carried by sea.

Article VIII. Limitation of liability [p. 54]

The provisions of these Rules shall not affect the rights and obligations of the carrier under any statute for the time being in force relating to the limitation of the liability of owners of sea-going vessels.

Article IX. Gold clause/nuclear exclusion [p. 54]

The monetary units mentioned in these Rules are to be taken to be gold value.

VISBY AMENDMENT—THE BRUSSELS PROTOCOL 1968

Protocol to amend the International Convention for the Unification of Certain Rules of Law relating to Bills of Lading, signed at Brussels on 25th August 1924

(Brussels, February 23rd, 1968)

The Contracting Parties,
Considering that it is desirable to amend the International Convention for the unification of certain rules of law relating to bills of lading, signed at Brussels on 25th August 1924,
Have agreed as follows:

Article 1 [p. 24 and p. 26]

1. In Article 3, paragraph 4, shall be added:

"However, proof to the contrary shall not be admissible when the bill of lading has been transferred to a third party acting in good faith."

2. In Article 3, paragraph 6, sub-paragraph 4 shall be deleted and replaced by:

"Subject to paragraph 6 *bis* the carrier and the ship shall in any event be discharged from all liability whatsoever in respect of the goods, unless suit is brought within one year of their delivery or of the date when they should have been delivered. This period may, however, be extended if the parties so agree after the cause of action has arisen."

3. In Article 3, after paragraph 6, shall be added the following paragraph 6 *bis*:

"An action for indemnity against a third person may be brought even after the expiration of the year provided for in the preceding paragraph if brought within the time allowed by the law of the Court seized of the case. However, the time allowed shall be not less than three months, commencing from the day when the person bringing such action for indemnity has settled the claim or has been served with process in the action against himself."

Article 2 [p. 42]

Article 4, paragraph 5, shall be deleted and replaced by the following:

"(*a*) Unless the nature and value of such goods have been declared by the shipper before shipment and inserted in the bill of lading, neither the carrier nor the ship shall in any event be or become liable for any loss or damage to or in connection with the goods in an amount exceeding the equivalent of 10.000 francs per package or unit or 30 francs per kilo of gross weight of the goods lost or damaged, whichever is the higher.

(*b*) The total amount recoverable shall be calculated by reference to the value of such goods at the place and time at which the goods are discharged from the ship in accordance with the contract or should have been so discharged.

The value of the goods shall be fixed according to the commodity exchange price, or, if there be no such price, according to the current market price, or, if there be no commodity exchange price or current market price, by reference to the normal value of goods of the same kind and quality.

(*c*) Where a container, pallet or similar article of transport is used to consolidate goods, the number of packages or units enumerated in the bill of lading as packed in such article of transport shall be deemed the number of packages or units for the purpose of this paragraph as far as these packages or units are concerned. Except as aforesaid such article of transport shall be considered the package or unit.

(*d*) A franc means a unit consisting of 65.6 milligrammes of gold of millesimal fineness 900'. The date of conversion of the sum awarded into national currencies shall be governed by the law of the Court seized of the case.

(*e*) Neither the carrier nor the ship shall be entitled to the benefit of the limitation of liability provided for in this paragraph if it is proved that the damage resulted from an act or omission of the carrier done with intent to cause damage, or recklessly and with knowledge that damage would probably result.

(*f*) The declaration mentioned in sub-paragraph (*a*) of this paragraph, if embodied in the bill of lading, shall be prima facie evidence, but shall not be binding or conclusive on the carrier.

(*g*) By agreement between the carrier, master or agent of the carrier and the shipper other maximum amounts than those mentioned in sub-paragraph (*a*) of this paragraph may be fixed, provided that no maximum amount so fixed shall be less than the appropriate maximum mentioned in that sub-paragraph.

(*h*) Neither the carrier nor the ship shall be responsible in any event for loss or damage to, or in connection with, goods if the nature or value thereof has been knowingly mis-stated by the shipper in the bill of lading."

Article 3 [p. 50]

Between Articles 4 and 5 of the Convention shall be inserted the following Article 4 *bis*:

"1. The defences and limits of liability provided for in this Convention shall apply in any action against the carrier in respect of loss or damage to goods covered by a contract of carriage whether the action be founded in contract or in tort.

2. If such an action is brought against a servant or agent of the carrier (such servant or agent not being an independent contractor), such servant or agent shall be entitled to avail himself of the defences and limits of liability which the carrier is entitled to invoke under this Convention.

3. The aggregate of the amounts recoverable from the carrier, and such servants and agents, shall in no case exceed the limit provided for in this Convention.

4. Nevertheless, a servant or agent of the carrier shall not be entitled to avail himself of the provisions of this Article, if it is proved that the damage resulted from an act or omission of the servant or agent done with intent to cause damage or recklessly and with knowledge that damage would probably result."

Article 4 [p. 54]

Article 9 of the Convention shall be deleted and replaced by the following:

"These Rules shall not affect the provisions of any international Convention or national law governing liability for nuclear damage."

Article 5 [p. 54]

Article 10 of the Convention shall be deleted and replaced by the following:

"The provisions of these Rules shall apply to every bill of lading relating to the carriage of goods between ports in two different States if:
  (a) the bill of lading is issued in a Contracting State, or
  (b) the carriage is from a port in a Contracting State, or
  (c) the Contract contained in or evidenced by the bill of lading provides that the rules of this Convention or legislation of any State giving effect to them are to govern the contract, whatever may be the nationality of the ship, the carrier, the shipper, the consignee, or any other interested person.
Each Contracting State shall apply the provisions of this Convention to the bills of lading mentioned above.

This Article shall not prevent a Contracting State from applying the Rules of this Convention to bills of lading not included in the preceding paragraphs."

Article 6

As between the Parties to this Protocol the Convention and the Protocol shall be read and interpreted together as one single instrument.

A Party to this Protocol shall have no duty to apply the provisions of this Protocol to bills of lading issued in a State which is a Party to the Convention but which is not a Party to this Protocol.

Article 7

As between the Parties to this Protocol, denunciation by any of them of the Convention in accordance with Article 15 thereof, shall not be construed in any way as a denunciation of the Convention as amended by this Protocol.

Article 8

Any dispute between two or more Contracting Parties concerning the interpretation or application of the Convention which cannot be settled through negotiation, shall, at the request of one of them, be submitted to arbitration. If within six months from the date of the request for arbitration the Parties are unable to agree on the organization of the arbitration, any one of those Parties may refer the dispute to the International Court of Justice by request in conformity with the Statute of the Court.

Article 9

1. Each Contracting Party may at the time of signature or ratification of this Protocol or accession thereto, declare that it does not consider itself bound by Article 8 of this Protocol. The other Contracting Parties shall not be bound by this Article with respect to any Contracting Party having made such a reservation.

2. Any Contracting Party having made a reservation in accordance with paragraph 1 may at any time withdraw this reservation by notification to the Belgian Government.

Article 10

This Protocol shall be open for signature by the States which have ratified the Convention or which have adhered thereto before the 23rd February 1968, and by any State represented at the twelfth session (1967–1968) of the Diplomatic Conference on Maritime Law.

Article 11

1. This Protocol shall be ratified.

2. Ratification of this Protocol by any State which is not a Party to the Convention shall have the effect of accession to the Convention.

3. The instruments of ratification shall be deposited with the Belgian Government.

Article 12

1. States, Members of the United Nations or Members of the specialized agencies of the United Nations, not represented at the twelfth session of the Diplomatic Conference on Maritime Law, may accede to this Protocol.

2. Accession to this Protocol shall have the effect of accession to the Convention.

3. The instruments of accession shall be deposited with the Belgian Government.

Article 13

1. This Protocol shall come into force three months after the date of the deposit of ten instruments of ratification or accession, of which at least five shall have been deposited by States that have each a tonnage equal or superior to one million gross tons of tonnage.

2. For each State which ratifies this Protocol or accedes thereto after the date of deposit of the instrument of ratification or accession determining the coming into force such as is stipulated in § 1 of this Article, this Protocol shall come into force three months after the deposit of its instrument of ratification or accession.

Article 14

1. Any Contracting State may denounce this Protocol by notification to the Belgian Government.

2. This denunciation shall have the effect of denunciation of the Convention.

3. The denunciation shall take effect one year after the date on which the notification has been received by the Belgian Government.

Article 15

1. Any Contracting State may at the time of signature, ratification or accession or at any time thereafter declare by written notification to the Belgian Government which among the territories under its sovereignty or for whose international relations it is responsible, are those to which the present Protocol applies.

The Protocol shall three months after the date of the receipt of such notification by the Belgian Government extend to the territories named therein, but not before the date of the coming into force of the Protocol in respect of such State.

2. This extension also shall apply to the Convention if the latter is not yet applicable to those territories.

3. Any Contracting State which has made a declaration under § 1 of this Article may at any time thereafter declare by notification given to the Belgian Government that the Protocol shall cease to extend to such territory. This denunciation shall take effect one year after the date on which notification thereof has been received by the Belgian Government; it also shall apply to the Convention.

Article 16

The Contracting Parties may give effect to this Protocol either by giving it the force of law or by including in their national legislation in a form appropriate to that legislation the rules adopted under this Protocol.

Article 17

The Belgian Government shall notify the States represented at the twelfth session (1967–1968) of the Diplomatic Conference on Maritime Law, the acceding States to this Protocol, and the States Parties to the Convention, of the following:

1. The signatures, ratifications and accessions received in accordance with Articles 10, 11 and 12.
2. The date on which the present Protocol will come into force in accordance with Article 13.
3. The notifications with regard to the territorial application in accordance with Article 15.
4. The denunciations received in accordance with Article 14.

In witness whereof the undersigned Plenipotentiaries, duly authorized, have signed this Protocol.

Done at Brussels, this 23rd day of February 1968, in the French and English languages, both texts being equally authentic, in a single copy, which shall remain deposited in the archives of the Belgian Government, which shall issue certified copies.

(*The signatures*)

HAGUE-VISBY RULES—CARRIAGE OF GOODS BY SEA ACT 1971 AS AMENDED BY THE MERCHANT SHIPPING ACT 1981 (SDR PROTOCOL)

An Act to amend the law with respect to the carriage of goods by sea.

[8 April 1971]

Be it enacted by the Queen's most Excellent Majesty, by and with the advice and consent of the Lords Spiritual and Temporal, and Commons, in this present Parliament assembled, and by the authority of the same, as follows:

Application of Hague Rules as amended [p. 9]

1.—(1) In this Act, "the Rules" means the International Convention for the unification of certain rules of law relating to bills of lading signed at Brussels on 25th August 1924, as amended by the Protocol signed at Brussels on 23rd February 1968 [and by the Protocol signed at Brussels on 21st December 1979].

(2) The provisions of the Rules, as set out in the Schedule to this Act, shall have the force of law.

(3) Without prejudice to subsection (2) above, the said provisions shall have effect (and have the force of law) in relation to and in connection with the carriage of goods by sea in ships where the port of shipment is a port in the United Kingdom, whether or not the carriage is between ports in two different States within the meaning of Article X of the Rules.

(4) Subject to subsection (6) below, nothing in this section shall be taken as applying anything in the Rules to any contract for the carriage of goods by sea, unless the contract expressly or by implication provides for the issue of a bill of lading or any similar document of title.

(5) The Secretary of State may from time to time by order made by statutory instrument specify the respective amounts which for the purposes of paragraph 5 of Article IV of the Rules and of Article IV *bis* of the Rules are to be taken as equivalent to the sums expressed in francs which are mentioned in sub-paragraph (a) of that paragraph.

(6) Without prejudice to Article X(*c*) of the rules, the Rules shall have the force of law in relation to—

(*a*)   any bill of lading if the contract contained in or evidenced by it expressly provides that the Rules shall govern the contract, and

(*b*)   any receipt which is a non-negotiable document marked as such if the contract contained in or evidenced by it is a contract for the carriage of goods by sea which expressly provides that the Rules are to govern the contract as if the receipt were a bill of lading,

but subject, where paragraph (*b*) applies, to any necessary modifications and in particular with the omission in Article III of the Rules of the second sentence of paragraph 4 and of paragraph 7.

(7) If and so far as the contract contained in or evidenced by a bill of lading or receipt within paragraph (*a*) or (*b*) of subsection (6) above applies to deck cargo or live animals, the Rules as given the force of law by that subsection shall have the effect as if Article 1(*c*) did not exclude deck cargo and live animals.

In this subsection "deck cargo" means cargo which by the contract of carriage is stated as being carried on deck and is so carried.

Contracting states, etc. [p. 11]

2.—(1) If Her Majesty by Order in Council certifies to the following effect, that is to say, that for the purposes of the Rules—

(a) a State specified in the Order is a contracting State, or is a contracting State in respect of any place or territory so specified; or

(b) any place or territory specified in the Order forms part of a State so specified (whether a contracting State or not),
the Order shall, except so far as it has been superseded by a subsequent Order, be conclusive evidence of the matters so certified.

(2) An Order in Council under this section may be varied or revoked by a subsequent Order in Council.

Absolute warranty of seaworthiness not to be implied in contracts to which Rules apply [p. 12]

3. There shall not be implied in any contract for the carriage of goods by sea to which the Rules apply by virtue of this Act any absolute undertaking by the carrier of the goods to provide a seaworthy ship.

Application of Act to British possessions, etc. [p. 12]

4.—(1) Her Majesty may by Order in Council direct that this Act shall extend, subject to such exceptions, adaptations and modifications as may be specified in the Order, to all or any of the following territories, that is—

(a) any colony (not being a colony for whose external relations a country other than the United Kingdom is responsible),

(b) any country outside Her Majesty's dominions in which Her Majesty has jurisdiction in right of Her Majesty's Government of the United Kingdom.

(2) An Order in Council under this section may contain such transitional and other consequential and incidental provisions as appear to Her Majesty to be expedient, including provisions amending or repealing any legislation about the carriage of goods by sea forming part of the law of any of the territories mentioned in paragraphs (a) and (b) above.

(3) An Order in Council under this section may be varied or revoked by a subsequent Order in Council.

Extension of application of Rules to carriage from ports in British possessions, etc. [p. 12]

5.—(1) Her Majesty may by Order in Council provide that section 1(3) of this Act shall have effect as if the reference therein to the United Kingdom included a reference to all or any of the following territories, that is—

(a) the Isle of Man;

   (*b*) any of the Channel Islands specified in the Order;

   (*c*) any colony specified in the Order (not being a colony for whose external relations a country other than the United Kingdom is responsible);

   (*d*) any associated state (as defined by section 1(3) of the West Indies Act 1967) specified in the Order;

   (*e*) any country specified in the Order, being a country outside Her Majesty's dominions in which Her Majesty has jurisdiction in right of Her Majesty's Government of the United Kingdom.

(2) An Order in Council under this section may be varied or revoked by a subsequent Order in Council.

Supplemental [p. 13]

6.—(1) This Act may be cited as the Carriage of Goods by Sea Act 1971.

(2) It is hereby declared that this Act extends to Northern Ireland.

(3) The following enactments shall be repealed, that is—

   (*a*) the Carriage of Goods by Sea Act 1924,

   (*b*) section 12(4)(*a*) of the Nuclear Installations Act 1965,

and without prejudice to section 38(1) of the Interpretation Act 1889, the reference to the said Act of 1924 in section 1(*1*)(i)(ii) of the Hovercraft Act 1968 shall include a reference to this Act.

(4) It is hereby declared that for the purposes of Article VIII of the Rules . . . [section 18 of the Merchant Shipping Act 1979 (which] entirely exempts shipowners and others in certain circumstances from liability for loss of, or damage to, goods) is a provision relating to limitation of liability.

(5) This Act shall come into force on such day as Her Majesty may by Order in Council appoint, and, for the purposes of the transition from the law in force immediately before the day appointed under this subsection to the provisions of this Act, the Order appointing the day may provide that those provisions shall have effect subject to such transitional provisions as may be contained in the Order.

SCHEDULE. THE HAGUE RULES AS AMENDED BY THE BRUSSELS PROTOCOL 1968

Article I. Definitions [p. 15]

In these Rules the following words are employed, with the meanings set out below:—

   (*a*) "Carrier" includes the owner or the charterer who enters into a contract of carriage with a shipper.

(b) "Contract of carriage" applies only to contracts of carriage covered by a bill of lading or any similar document of title, in so far as such document relates to the carriage of goods by sea, including any bill of lading or any similar document as aforesaid issued under or pursuant to a charter-party from the moment at which such bill of lading or similar document of title regulates the relations between a carrier and a holder of the same.

(c) "Goods" includes goods, wares, merchandise, and articles of every kind whatsoever except live animals and cargo which by the contract of carriage is stated as being carried on deck and is so carried.

(d) "Ship" means any vessel used for the carriage of goods by sea.

(e) "Carriage of goods" covers the period from the time when the goods are loaded on to the time they are discharged from the ship.

Article II. Risks [p. 19]

Subject to the provisions of Article VI, under every contract of carriage of goods by sea the carrier, in relation to the loading, handling, stowage, carriage, custody, care and discharge of such goods, shall be subject to the responsibilities and liabilities, and entitled to the rights and immunities hereinafter set forth.

Article III. Responsibilities and liabilities [p. 19]

1. The carrier shall be bound before and at the beginning of the voyage to exercise due diligence to—
   (a) Make the ship seaworthy.
   (b) Properly man, equip and supply the ship.
   (c) Make the holds, refrigerating and cool chambers, and all other parts of the ship in which goods are carried, fit and safe for their reception, carriage and preservation.

2. Subject to the provisions of Article IV, the carrier shall properly and carefully load, handle, stow, carry, keep, care for, and discharge the goods carried.

(3) After receiving the goods into his charge the carrier or the master or agent of the carrier shall, on demand of the shipper, issue to the shipper a bill of lading showing among other things—

(a) The leading marks necessary for identification of the goods as the same are furnished in writing by the shipper before the loading of such goods starts, provided such marks are stamped or otherwise shown clearly upon the goods if uncovered, or on the cases or coverings in which such goods are contained, in such a manner as should ordinarily remain legible until the end of the voyage.

(*b*) Either the number of packages or pieces, or the quantity, or weight, as the case may be, as furnished in writing by the shipper.

(*c*) The apparent order and condition of the goods.

Provided that no carrier, master or agent of the carrier shall be bound to state or show in the bill of lading any marks, number, quantity, or weight which he has reasonable ground for suspecting not accurately to represent the goods actually received, or which he has had no reasonable means of checking.

4. Such a bill of lading shall be *prima facie* evidence of the receipt by the carrier of the goods as therein described in accordance with paragraph 3(*a*), (*b*) and (*c*). However, proof to the contrary shall not be admissible when the bill of lading has been transferred to a third party acting in good faith.

5. The shipper shall be deemed to have guaranteed to the carrier the accuracy at the time of shipment of the marks, number, quantity and weight, as furnished by him, and the shipper shall indemnify the carrier against all loss, damages and expenses arising or resulting from inaccuracies in such particulars. The right of the carrier to such indemnity shall in no way limit his responsibility and liability under the contract of carriage to any person other than the shipper.

6. Unless notice of loss or damage and the general nature of such loss or damage be given in writing to the carrier or his agent at the port of discharge before or at the time of the removal of the goods into the custody of the person entitled to delivery thereof under the contract of carriage, or, if the loss or damage be not apparent, within three days, such removal shall be prima facie evidence of the delivery by the carrier of the goods as described in the bill of lading.

The notice in writing need not be given if the state of the goods has, at the time of their receipt, been the subject of joint survey or inspection.

Subject to paragraph 6 *bis* the carrier and the ship shall in any event be discharged from all liability whatsoever in respect of the goods, unless suit is brought within one year of their delivery or of the date when they should have been delivered. This period may, however, be extended if the parties so agree after the cause of action has arisen.

In the case of any actual or apprehended loss or damage the carrier and the receiver shall give all reasonable facilities to each other for inspecting and tallying the goods.

6 *bis*. An action for indemnity against a third person may be brought even after the expiration of the year provided for in the preceding paragraph if brought within the time allowed by the law of the Court seized of the case. However, the time allowed shall be not less than three months, commencing from the day when the person bringing such action for indemnity has settled the claim or has been served with process in the action against himself.

7. After the goods are loaded the bill of lading to be issued by the carrier, master, or agent of the carrier, to the shipper shall, if the shipper so demands, be a "shipped" bill of lading, provided that if the shipper shall have previously

taken up any document of title to such goods, he shall surrender the same as against the issue of the "shipped" bill of lading, but at the option of the carrier such document of title may be noted at the port of shipment by the carrier, master, or agent with the name or names of the ship or ships upon which the goods have been shipped and the date or dates of shipment, and when so noted, if it shows the particulars mentioned in paragraph 3 of Article III shall for the purposes of this article be deemed to constitute a "shipped" bill of lading.

8. Any clause, covenant, or agreement in a contract of carriage relieving the carrier or the ship from liability for loss or damage to, or in connection with, goods arising from negligence, fault, or failure in the duties and obligations provided in this article or lessening such liability otherwise than as provided in these Rules, shall be null and void and of no effect. A benefit of insurance in favour of the carrier or similar clause shall be deemed to be a clause relieving the carrier from liability.

Article IV. Rights and immunities [p. 31]

1. Neither the carrier nor the ship shall be liable for loss or damage arising or resulting from unseaworthiness unless caused by want of due diligence on the part of the carrier to make the ship seaworthy, and to secure that the ship is properly manned, equipped and supplied, and to make the holds, refrigerating and cool chambers and all other parts of the ship in which goods are carried fit and safe for their reception, carriage and preservation in accordance with the provisions of paragraph 1 of Article III. Whenever loss or damage has resulted from unseaworthiness the burden of proving the exercise of due diligence shall be on the carrier or other person claiming exception under this article.

2. Neither the carrier nor the ship shall be responsible for loss or damage arising or resulting from— .

   (a) Act, neglect, or default of the master, mariner, pilot, or the servants of the carrier in the navigation or in the management of the ship.

   (b) Fire, unless caused by the actual fault or privity of the carrier.

   (c) Perils, dangers and accidents of the sea or other navigable waters.

   (d) Act of God.

   (e) Act of war.

   (f) Act of public enemies.

   (g) Arrest or restraint of princes, rulers or people, or seizure under legal process.

   (h) Quarantine restrictions.

   (i) Act or omission of the shipper or owner of the goods, his agent or representative.

   (j) Strikes or lockouts or stoppage or restraint of labour from whatever cause, whether partial or general.

(*k*) Riots and civil commotions.

(*l*) Saving or attempting to save life or property at sea.

(*m*) Wastage in bulk or weight or any other loss or damage arising from inherent defect, quality or vice of the goods.

(*n*) Insufficiency of packing.

(*o*) Insufficiency or inadequacy of marks.

(*p*) Latent defects not discoverable by due diligence.

(*q*) Any other cause arising without the actual fault or privity of the carrier, or without the fault or neglect of the agents or servants of the carrier, but the burden of proof shall be on the person claiming the benefit of this exception to show that neither the actual fault or privity of the carrier nor the fault or neglect of the agents or servants of the carrier contributed to the loss or damage.

3. The shipper shall not be responsible for loss or damage sustained by the carrier or the ship arising or resulting from any cause without the act, fault or neglect of the shipper, his agents or his servants.

4. Any deviation in saving or attempting to save life or property at sea or any reasonable deviation shall not be deemed to be infringement or breach of these Rules or of the contract of carriage, and the carrier shall not be liable for any loss or damage resulting therefrom.

5.(*a*) Unless the nature and value of such goods have been declared by the shipper before shipment and inserted in the bill of lading, neither the carrier nor the ship shall in any event be or become liable for any loss or damage to or in connection with the goods in an amount exceeding [666.67 units of account] per package or unit or [2 units of account per kilogramme] of gross weight of the goods lost or damaged, whichever is the higher.

(*b*) The total amount recoverable shall be calculated by reference to the value of such goods at the place and time at which the goods are discharged from the ship in accordance with the contract or should have been so discharged.

The value of the goods shall be fixed according to the commodity exchange price, or, if there be no such price, according to the current market price, or, if there be no commodity exchange price or current market price, by reference to the normal value of goods of the same kind and quality.

(*c*) Where a container, pallet or similar article of transport is used to consolidate goods, the number of packages or units enumerated in the bill of lading as packed in such article of transport shall be deemed the number of packages or units for the purpose of this paragraph as far as these packages or units are concerned. Except as aforesaid such article of transport shall be considered the package or unit.

[(*d*) The unit of account mentioned in this Article is the special drawing right as defined by the International Monetary Fund. The amounts mentioned in sub-paragraph (*a*) of this paragraph shall be converted into national currency on the basis of the value of that currency on a date to be determined by the law of the Court seized of the case.]

(*e*) Neither the carrier nor the ship shall be entitled to the benefit of the limitation of liability provided for in this paragraph if it is proved that the damage resulted from an act or omission of the carrier done with intent to cause damage, or recklessly and with knowledge that damage would probably result.

(*f*) The declaration mentioned in sub-paragraph (*a*) of this paragraph, if embodied in the bill of lading, shall be prima facie evidence, but shall not be binding or conclusive on the carrier.

(*g*) By agreement between the carrier, master or agent of the carrier and the shipper other maximum amounts than those mentioned in sub-paragraph (*a*) of this paragraph may be fixed, provided that no maximum amount so fixed shall be less than the appropriate maximum mentioned in that sub-paragraph.

(*h*) Neither the carrier nor the ship shall be responsible in any event for loss or damage to, or in connection with, goods if the nature or value thereof has been knowingly mis-stated by the shipper in the bill of lading.

6. Goods of an inflammable, explosive or dangerous nature to the shipment whereof the carrier, master or agent of the carrier has not consented with knowledge of their nature and character, may at any time before discharge be landed at any place, or destroyed or rendered innocuous by the carrier without compensation and the shipper of such goods shall be liable for all damages and expenses directly or indirectly arising out of or resulting from such shipment. If any such goods shipped with such knowledge and consent shall become a danger to the ship or cargo, they may in like manner be landed at any place, or destroyed or rendered innocuous by the carrier without liability on the part of the carrier except to general average, if any.

Article IV. *bis* [p. 50]

1. The defences and limits of liability provided for in these Rules shall apply in any action against the carrier in respect of loss or damage to goods covered by a contract of carriage whether the action be founded in contract or in tort.

2. If such an action is brought against a servant or agent of the carrier (such servant or agent not being an independent contractor), such servant or agent shall be entitled to avail himself of the defences and limits of liability which the carrier is entitled to invoke under these Rules.

3. The aggregate of the amounts recoverable from the carrier, and such servants and agents, shall in no case exceed the limit provided for in these Rules.

4. Nevertheless, a servant or agent of the carrier shall not be entitled to avail himself of the provisions of this article, if it is proved that the damage resulted from an act or omission of the servant or agent done with intent to cause

damage or recklessly and with knowledge that damage would probably result.

Article V. Surrender of rights and immunities, and increase of responsibilities and liabilities [p. 51]

A carrier shall be at liberty to surrender in whole or in part all or any of his rights and immunities or to increase any of his responsibilities and obligations under these Rules, provided such surrender or increase shall be embodied in the bill of lading issued to the shipper. The provisions of these Rules shall not be applicable to charterparties, but if bills of lading are issued in the case of a ship under a charterparty they shall comply with the terms of these Rules. Nothing in these Rules shall be held to prevent the insertion in a bill of lading of any lawful provisions regarding general average.

Article VI. Special conditions [p. 52]

Notwithstanding the provisions of the preceding articles, a carrier, master or agent of the carrier and a shipper shall in regard to any particular goods be at liberty to enter into any agreement in any terms as to the responsibility and liability of the carrier for such goods, and as to the rights and immunities of the carrier in respect of such goods, or his obligation as to seaworthiness, so far as this stipulation is not contrary to public policy, or the care or diligence of his servants or agents in regard to the loading, handling, stowage, carriage, custody, care and discharge of the goods carried by sea, provided that in this case no bill of lading has been or shall be issued and that the terms agreed shall be embodied in a receipt which shall be a non-negotiable document and shall be marked as such.

Any agreement so entered into shall have full legal effect.

Provided that this article shall not apply to ordinary commercial shipments made in the ordinary course of trade, but only to other shipments where the character or condition of the property to be carried or the circumstances, terms and conditions under which the carriage is to be performed are such as reasonably to justify a special agreement.

Article VII. Limitations on the application of the Rules [p. 53]

Nothing herein contained shall prevent a carrier or a shipper from entering into any agreement, stipulation, condition, reservation or exemption as to the responsibility and liability of the carrier or the ship for the loss or damage to, or in connection with, the custody and care and handling of goods prior to the loading on, and subsequent to the discharge from, the ship on which the goods are carried by sea.

Article VIII. Limitation of liability [p. 54]

The provisions of these Rules shall not affect the rights and obligations of the carrier under any statute for the time being in force relating to the limitation of the liability of owners of sea-going vessels.

Article IX. Nuclear exclusion [p. 54]

These Rules shall not affect the provisions of any international Convention or national law governing liability for nuclear damage.

Article X. Application [p. 54]

The provisions of these Rules shall apply to every bill of lading relating to the carriage of goods between ports in two different States if:

(*a*) the bill of lading is issued in a contracting State, or

(*b*) the carriage is from a port in a contracting State, or

(*c*) the contract contained in or evidenced by the bill of lading provides that these Rules or legislation of any State giving effect to them are to govern the contract,

whatever may be the nationality of the ship, the carrier, the shipper, the consignee, or any other interested person.

[The last two paragraphs of this article are not reproduced. They require contracting States to apply the Rules to bills of lading mentioned in the article and authorise them to apply the Rules to other bills of lading.]

[Articles 11 to 16 of the International Convention for the unification of certain rules of law relating to bills of lading signed at Brussels on 25th August 1924 are not reproduced. They deal with the coming into force of the Convention, procedure for ratification, accession and denunciation, and the right to call for a fresh conference to consider amendments to the Rules contained in the Convention.]

COUNTRIES WITH LEGISLATION APPLYING THE HAGUE RULES AND HAGUE-VISBY RULES

Warning

Any lists of this nature will always be a matter of opinion and interpretation. An easy (but not particularly helpful to the practitioner) approach is to produce "official" lists of those who have deposited documents of accession or ratification of the relevant Rules which have not been denounced in favour of some other Rules. This approach ignores completely that many countries do not bother to denounce one set of Rules before adopting another whilst others (for a variety of reasons) enact Rules into national legislation without bothering to accede or ratify the International Convention in which they appear. Other countries tinker with the Rules in enacting them, thereby adding to the confusion of international lack of uniformity (*see* Appendix V) whilst other countries merge, fragment, change name or take a myriad of other steps designed to frustrate efforts to produce a comprehensive, accurate list for practitioners.

The purpose of these lists is to attempt to indicate what Rules are presently applied in the courts of the countries indicated regardless of what Rules they may have acceded to, ratified or denounced. It is impossible to vouch for the total accuracy of such lists but the author feels that, to a practitioner, this type of list is of greater value than an official list of signatories. Whilst every effort has been made to make it accurate, it should be used as a guide only and local contemporary advice should be sought where confirmed accurate data is required at any given time.

N.B.: Those nations that have neither ratified or acceded are marked*.

HAGUE RULES

Algeria

Angola

Anguilla

Antigua & Barbuda

Argentina[1]

Ascension Island and St. Helena

Bahamas

Belize

1. Hague-Visby adopted in part.

Bolivia
Cape Verde Islands
Croatia
Cuba
Cyprus
Dominican Republic
Fiji
Ghana
Goa
Grenada
Guyana
Iran
Ireland
Ivory Coast
Jamaica
Kenya
Kiribati
Kuwait
Macau
Madagascar
Malaysia
Mauritius
Monaco
Mozambique
Nauru

*Pakistan
*Panama
Papua New Guinea
Paraguay
Peru
*Philippines
Portugal
*Sabah
Sao Tomé
Sarawak
Seychelles
*Slovenia
Solomon Islands
Somalia
St Kitts-Nevis
St Lucia
*St Martin
St Vincent & Grenadines
*Taiwan
Timor
Trinidad & Tobago
Turkey
Tuvalu
United States of America
Zaire

HAGUE-VISBY RULES

Australia
Belgium
Bermuda
*Canada
Cayman Islands
Denmark
Ecuador
*Egypt[1]
Finland
France
*Germany

Gibraltar
Greece
Hong Kong
*Iceland
*India[2]
*Israel
Italy
Japan
Liberia
Luxembourg
Mexico

1. Due to adopt Hamburg Rules with effect from 1 November 1998.
2. Under Multimodal Transportation of Goods Ordinance 1992 Part II of the Schedule amends the 1925 Indian COGSA to apply Hague-Visby to port-to-port carriage but not multimodal.

Montserrat
Netherlands
New Zealand
*Oman
Poland
Singapore
*South Africa
Spain
Sri Lanka

Sweden
Switzerland
Syria
Tonga
Turks & Caicos Islands
United Kingdom[3]
UK Virgin Islands
*Vietnam

Additionally China, Korea, Thailand and the United Arab Emirates apply legislation which is largely Hague-Visby based.

The situation in Russia and former Soviet Union (FSU) states is unclear.

HAGUE-VISBY SDR PROTOCOL

Australia
Belgium
Bermuda
*Canada
Cayman Islands
Denmark
*Egypt
Finland
France
*Germany
Georgia
Gibraltar
Greece
Hong Kong
*Iceland
*India
*Israel
Italy

Japan
*Liberia
Luxembourg
Mexico
Montserrat
Netherlands
New Zealand
Norway
*Oman
Poland
*South Africa
Spain
Sweden
Switzerland
Turks & Caicos Islands
United Kingdom[3]
UK Virgin Islands

3. Includes British Antarctic Territory, Falkland Islands and Isle of Man.

THE YORK-ANTWERP RULES 1994

Rule of interpretation

In the adjustment of general average the following rules shall apply to the exclusion of any Law and Practice inconsistent therewith.

Except as provided by the Rule Paramount and the numbered Rules, general average shall be adjusted according to the lettered Rules.

Rule paramount

In no case shall there be any allowance for sacrifice or expenditure unless reasonably made or incurred.

Rule A

There is a general average act when, and only when, any extraordinary sacrifice or expenditure is intentionally and reasonably made or incurred for the common safety for the purpose of preserving from peril the property involved in a common maritime adventure.

General average sacrifices and expenditures shall be borne by the different contributing interests on the basis hereinafter provided.

Rule B

There is a common maritime adventure when one or more vessels are towing or pushing another vessel or vessels, provided that they are all involved in commercial activities and not in a salvage operation.

When measures are taken to preserve the vessels and their cargoes, if any, from a common peril, these Rules shall apply.

A vessel is not in common peril with another vessel or vessels if by simply disconnecting from the other vessel or vessels she is in safety; but if the disconnection is itself a general average act the common maritime adventure continues.

Rule C

Only such losses, damages or expenses which are the direct consequence of the general average act shall be allowed as general average.

In no case shall there be any allowance in general average for losses, damages or expenses incurred in respect of damage to the environment or in consequence of the escape or release of pollutant substances from the property involved in the common maritime adventure.

Demurrage, loss of market, and any loss or damage sustained or expense incurred by reason of delay, whether on the voyage or subsequently, and any indirect loss whatsoever, shall not be admitted as general average.

Rule D

Rights to contribution in general average shall not be affected, though the event which gave rise to the sacrifice or expenditure may have been due to the fault of one of the parties to the adventure, but this shall not prejudice any remedies or defences which may be open against or to that party in respect of such fault.

Rule E

The onus of proof is upon the party claiming in general average to show that the loss or expense claimed is properly allowable as general average.

All parties claiming in general average shall give notice in writing to the average adjuster of the loss or expense in respect of which they claim contribution within 12 months of the date of the termination of the common maritime adventure.

Failing such notification, or if within 12 months of a request for the same any of the parties shall fail to supply evidence in support of a notified claim, or particulars of value in respect of a contributory interest, the average adjuster shall be at liberty to estimate the extent of the allowance or the contributory value on the basis of the information available to him, which estimate may be challenged only on the ground that it is manifestly incorrect.

Rule F

Any additional expense incurred in place of another expense which would have been allowable as general average shall be deemed to be general average and so allowed without regard to the saving, if any, to other interests, but only up to the amount of the general average expense avoided.

Rule G

General average shall be adjusted as regards both loss and contribution upon the basis of values of the time and place when and where the adventure ends.

This rule shall not affect the determination of the place of which the average statement is to be made up.

When a ship is at any port or place in circumstances which would give rise to an allowance in general average under the provisions of Rules X and XI, and the cargo or part thereof is forwarded to destination by other means, rights and liabilities in general average shall, subject to cargo interests being notified if practicable, remain as nearly as possible the same as they would have been in the absence of such forwarding, as if the adventure had continued in the original ship for so long as justifiable under the contract of affreightment and the applicable law.

The proportion attaching to cargo of the allowances made in general average by reason of applying the third paragraph of this Rule shall not exceed the cost which would have been borne by the owners of cargo if the cargo had been forwarded at their expense.

Rule I. Jettison of cargo

No jettison of cargo shall be made good as general average, unless such cargo is carried in accordance with the recognised custom of the trade.

Rule II. Loss or damage by sacrifices for the common safety

Loss of or damage to the property involved in the common maritime adventure by or in consequence of a sacrifice made for the common safety, and by water which goes down a ship's hatches opened or other opening made for the purpose of making a jettison for the common safety, shall be made good as general average.

Rule III. Extinguishing fire on shipboard

Damage done to a ship and cargo, or either of them, by water or otherwise, including damage by beaching or scuttling a burning ship, in extinguishing a fire on board the ship, shall be made good as general average; except that no compensation shall be made for damage by smoke however caused or by heat of the fire.

Rule IV. Cutting away wreck

Loss or damage sustained by cutting away wreck or parts of the ship which have been previously carried away or are effectively lost by accident shall not be made good as general average.

Rule V. Voluntary stranding

When a ship is intentionally run on shore for the common safety, whether or not she might have been driven on shore, the consequent loss or damage to the property involved in the common maritime adventure shall be allowed in general average.

Rule VI. Salvage remuneration

(a) Expenditure incurred by the parties to the adventure in the nature of salvage, whether under contract or otherwise, shall be allowed in general average provided that the salvage operations were carried out for the purpose of preserving from peril the property involved in the common maritime adventure.

Expenditure allowed in general average shall include any salvage remuneration in which the skill and efforts of the salvors in preventing or minimising damage to the environment such as is referred to in Art. 13 paragraph 1(b) of the International Convention on Salvage, 1989 have been taken into account.

(b) Special compensation payable to a salvor by the shipowner under Art. 14 of the said Convention to the extent specified in paragraph 4 of that Article or under any other provision similar in substance shall not be allowed in general average.

Rule VII. Damage to machinery and boilers

Damage caused to any machinery and boilers of a ship which is ashore and in a position of peril, in endeavouring to refloat, shall be allowed in general average when shown to have arisen from an actual intention to float the ship for the common safety at the risk of such damage; but where a ship is afloat no loss or damage caused by working the propelling machinery and boilers shall in any circumstances be made good as general average.

Rule VIII. Expenses lightening a ship when ashore, and consequent damage

When a ship is ashore and cargo and ship's fuel and stores or any of them are discharged as a general average act, the extra cost of lightening, lighter hire and reshipping (in incurred), and any loss or damage to the property involved in the common maritime adventure in consequence thereof, shall be admitted as general average.

Rule IX. Cargo, ship's materials and stores used for fuel

Cargo, ship's materials and stores, or any of them, necessarily used for fuel for the common safety at a time of peril shall be admitted as general average, but when such an allowance is made for the cost of ship's materials and stores the general average shall be credited with the estimated cost of the fuel which would otherwise have been consumed in prosecuting the intended voyage.

Rule X. Expenses at port of refuge, etc.

(a) When a ship shall have entered a port or place of refuge or shall have returned to her port or place of loading in consequence of accident, sacrifice or other extraordinary circumstances which render that necessary for the common safety, the expenses of entering such port or place shall be admitted as general average; and when she shall have sailed thence with her original cargo, or a part of it, the corresponding expenses of leaving such port or place consequent upon such entry or return shall likewise be admitted as general average.

When a ship is at any port or place of refuge and is necessarily removed to another port or place because repairs cannot be carried out in the first port or place, the provisions of this Rule shall be applied to the second port or place as if it were a port or place of refuge and the cost of such removal including temporary repairs and towage shall be admitted as general average. The provisions of Rule XI shall be applied to the prolongation of the voyage occasioned by such removal.

(b) The cost of handling on board or discharging cargo, fuel or stores whether at a port or place of loading, call or refuge, shall be admitted as general average, when the handling or discharge was necessary for the common safety or to enable damage to the ship caused by sacrifice or accident to be repaired, if the repairs were necessary for the safe prosecution of the voyage, except in cases where the damage to the ship is discovered at a port or place of loading or call without any accident or other extraordinary circumstances connected with such damage having taken place during the voyage.

The cost of handling on board or discharging cargo, fuel or stores shall not be admissible as general average when incurred solely for the purpose of restowage due to shifting during the voyage, unless such restowage is necessary for the common safety.

(c) Whenever the cost of handling or discharging cargo, fuel or stores is admissible as general average, the costs of storage, including insurance if reasonably incurred, reloading and stowing of such cargo, fuel or stores shall likewise be admitted as general average. The provisions of Rule XI shall be applied to the extra period of detention occasioned by such reloading or restowing.

But when the ship is condemned or does not proceed on her original voyage, storage expenses shall be admitted as general average only up to the date of the ship's condemnation or of the abandonment of the voyage or up to the date of completion of discharge of cargo if the condemnation or abandonment takes place before that date.

Rule XI. Wages and maintenance of crew and other expenses bearing up for and in a port of refuge, etc.

(a) Wages and maintenance of master, officers and crew reasonably incurred and fuel and stores consumed during the prolongation of the voyage occasioned by a ship entering a port or place of refuge or returning to her port or place of loading shall be admitted as general average when the expenses of entering such port or place are allowable in general average in accordance with Rule X(a).

(b) When a ship shall have entered or been detained in any port or place in consequence of accident, sacrifice or other extraordinary circumstances which render that necessary for the common safety, or to enable damage to the ship caused by sacrifice or accident to be repaired, if the repairs were necessary for the safe prosecution of the voyage, the wages and maintenance of the master, officers and crew reasonably incurred during the extra period of detention in such port or place until the ship shall or should have been made ready to proceed upon her voyage, shall be admitted in general average.

Fuel and stores consumed during the extra period of detention shall be admitted as general average, except such fuel and stores as are consumed in effecting repairs not allowable in general average.

Port charges incurred during the extra period of detention shall likewise be admitted as general average except such charges as are incurred solely by reason of repairs not allowable in general average.

Provided that when damage to the ship is discovered at a port or place of loading or call without any accident or other extraordinary circumstances connected with such damage having taken place during the voyage, then the wages, and maintenance of master, officers and crew and fuel and stores consumed and port charges incurred during the extra detention for repairs to damages so discovered shall not be admissible as general average, even if the repairs are necessary for the safe prosecution of the voyage.

When the ship is condemned or does not proceed on her original voyage, the wages and maintenance of the master, officers and crew and fuel and stores consumed and port charges shall be admitted as general average only up to the date of the ship's condemnation or of the abandonment of the voyage or up to the date of completion of discharge of cargo if the condemnation or abandonment takes place before that date.

(c) For the purpose of this and the other Rules wages shall include all payments made to or for the benefit of the master, officers and crew, whether such payments be imposed by law upon the shipowners or be made under the terms of articles of employment.

(d) The cost of measures undertaken to prevent or minimise damage to the environment shall be allowed in general average when incurred in any or all of the following circumstances:

   (i) as part of an operation performed for the common safety which, had it been undertaken by a party outside the common maritime adventure, would have entitled such party to a salvage reward;

  (ii) as a condition of entry into or departure from any port or place in the circumstances prescribed in rule X(a);

 (iii) as a condition of remaining at any port or place in the circumstances prescribed in Rule X(a) provided that when there is an actual escape or release of pollutant substances the cost of any additional measures required on that account to prevent or minimise pollution or environmental damage shall not be allowed as general average;

 (iv) necessarily in connection with the discharging, storing or reloading of cargo whenever the cost of those operations is admissible as general average.

Rule XII. Damage to cargo in discharging, etc.

Damage to or loss of cargo, fuel or stores sustained in consequence of their handling, discharging, storing, reloading and stowing shall be made good as general average, when and only when the cost of those measures respectively is admitted as general average.

Rule XIII. Deductions from cost of repairs

Repairs to be allowed in general average shall not be subject to deductions in respect of "new for old" where old material or parts are replaced by new unless the ship is over fifteen years old in which case there shall be a deduction of one third. The deductions shall be regulated by the age of the ship from the 31st December of the year of completion of construction to the date of the general average act, except for insulation, life and similar boats, communications and navigational apparatus and equipment, machinery and boilers for which the deductions shall be regulated by the age of the particular parts to which they apply.

    The deductions shall be made only from the cost of the new material or parts when finished and ready to be installed in the ship.

    No deduction shall be made in respect of provisions, stores, anchors and chain cables.

    Drydock and slipway dues and costs of shifting the ship shall be allowed in full.

    The costs of cleaning, painting or coating of bottom shall not be allowed in general average unless the bottom has been painted or coated within the twelve months preceding the date of the general average act in which case one half of such costs shall be allowed.

Rule XIV. Temporary repairs

Where temporary repairs are effected to a ship at a port of loading, call or refuge, for the common safety, or of damage caused by general average sacrifice, the cost of such repairs shall be admitted as general average.

Where temporary repairs of accidental damage are effected in order to enable the adventure to be completed, the cost of such repairs shall be admitted as general average without regard to the saving, if any, to other interests, but only up to the saving in expense which would have been incurred and allowed in general average if such repairs had not been effected there.

No deductions "new for old" shall be made from the cost of temporary repairs allowable as general average.

Rule XV. Loss of freight

Loss of freight arising from damage to or loss or cargo shall be made good as general average, either when caused by a general average act, or whom the damage to or loss of cargo is so made good.

Deduction shall be made from the amount of gross freight lost, of the charges which the owner thereof would have incurred to earn such freight, but has, in consequence of the sacrifice, not incurred.

Rule XVI. Amount to be made good for cargo lost or damaged by sacrifice

The amount to be made good as general average for damage to or loss or cargo sacrificed shall be the loss which has been sustained thereby based on the value at the time of discharge, ascertained from the commercial invoice rendered to the receiver or if there is no such invoice from the shipped value. The value at the time of discharge shall include the cost of insurance and freight except insofar as such freight is at the risk of interests other than the cargo.

When cargo so damaged is sold and the amount of the damage has not been otherwise agreed, the loss to be made good in general average shall be the difference between the net proceeds of sale and the net sound value as computed in the first paragraph of this Rule.

Rule XVII. Contributory values

The contribution to a general average shall be made upon the actual values of the property at the termination of the adventure except that the value of cargo shall be the value at the time of discharge, ascertained from the commercial invoice rendered to the receiver or if there is no such invoice from the shipped value. The value of the cargo shall include the cost of insurance and freight unless and insofar as such freight is at the risk of interests other than the cargo, deducting therefrom any loss or damage suffered by the cargo prior to or at the time of discharge. The value of the ship shall be assessed without taking into account the beneficial or detrimental effect of any demise or time charterparty to which the ship may be committed.

To these values shall be added the amount made good as general average for property sacrificed, if not already included, deduction being made from the freight and passage money at risk of such charges and crew's wages as would not have been incurred in earning the freight had the ship and cargo been totally lost at the date of the general average act and have not been allowed as general average; deduction being also made from the value of the property of all extra charges incurred in respect thereof subsequently to the general average act, except such charges as are allowed in general average or fall upon the ship by virtue of an award for special compensation under Art. 14 of the International Convention on Salvage, 1989 or under any other provision similar in substance.

In the circumstances envisaged in the third paragraph of Rule G, the cargo and other property shall contribute on the basis of its value upon delivery at original destination unless sold or otherwise disposed of short of that destination, and the ship shall contribute upon its actual net value at the time of completion of discharge of cargo.

Where cargo is sold short of destination, however, it shall contribute upon the actual net proceeds of sale, with the addition of any amount made good as general average.

Mails, passengers' luggage, personal effects and accompanied private motor vehicles shall not contribute in general average.

Rule XVIII. Damage to ship

The amount to be allowed as general average for damage or loss to the ship, her machinery and/or gear caused by a general average act shall be as follows:

(a) When repaired or replaced,
The actual reasonable cost of repairing or replacing such damage or loss, subject to deductions in accordance with Rule XIII;

(b) When not repaired or replaced,
The reasonable depreciation arising from such damage or loss, but not exceeding the estimated cost of repairs. But where the ship is an actual total loss or when the cost of repairs of the damage would exceed the value of the ship when repaired, the amount to be allowed as general average shall be the difference between the estimated sound value of the ship after deducing therefrom the estimated cost of repairing damage which is not general average

and the value of the ship in her damaged state which may be measured by the net proceeds of sale, if any.

Rule XIX. Undeclared or wrongfully declared cargo

Damage or loss caused to goods loaded without the knowledge of the ship-owner or his agent or to goods wilfully misdescribed at time of shipment shall not be allowed as general average, but such goods shall remain liable to contribute, if saved.

Damage or loss caused to goods which have been wrongfully declared on shipment at a value which is lower than their real value shall be contributed for at the declared value, but such goods shall contribute upon their actual value.

Rule XX. Provision of funds

A commission of 2 per cent. on general average disbursements other than the wages and maintenance of master, officers and crew and fuel and stores not replaced during the voyage, shall be allowed in general average.

The capital loss sustained by the owners of goods sold for the purpose of raising funds to defray general average disbursements shall be allowed in general average.

The cost of insuring general average disbursements shall also be admitted in general average.

Rule XXI. Interest on losses made good in general average

Interest shall be allowed on expenditure, sacrifices and allowances in general average at the rate of 7 per cent. per annum, until three months after the date of issue of the general average adjustment, due allowance being made for any payment on account by the contributory interests or from the general average deposit fund.

Rule XXII. Treatment of cash deposits

Where cash deposits have been collected in respect of cargo's liability for general average, salvage or special charges such deposits shall be paid without any delay into a special account in the joint names of a representative nominated on behalf of the shipowner and a representative nominated on behalf of the depositors in a bank to be approved by both. The sum so deposited together with accrued interest, if any, shall be held as security for payment to the parties entitled thereto of the general average, salvage or special charges payable by cargo in respect of which the deposits have been collected. Payments on account or refunds of deposits may be made if certified to in writing by the average adjuster. Such deposits and payments or refunds shall be without prejudice to the ultimate liability of the parties.

LOF 1995

LLOYD'S STANDARD FORM OF SALVAGE AGREEMENT — LOF 1995

LOF 1995

LLOYD'S

	NOTES
	1 Insert name of person signing on behalf of Owners of property to be salved. The Master should sign wherever possible
	2 The Contractor's name should always be inserted in line 4 and whenever the Agreement is signed by the Master of the Salving vessel or other person on behalf of the Contractor the name of the Master or other person must also be inserted in line 1 before the words "for and on behalf of". The words "for and on behalf of" should be deleted where a Contractor signs personally
STANDARD FORM OF	*3 Insert place if agreed in clause 1(a)(i) and currency if agreed in clause 1(e)*

SALVAGE AGREEMENT

(APPROVED AND PUBLISHED BY THE COUNCIL OF LLOYD'S)

NO CURE - NO PAY

On board the...
Dated....................................

* See Note 1 above

IT IS HEREBY AGREED between Captain+...
for and on behalf of the Owners of the ".." her
cargo freight bunkers stores and any other property thereon (hereinafter collectively called "the Owners")
and..for and on behalf of ....

* See Note 2 above

....(hereinafter called "the Contractor"*) that:-

1.   (a) The Contractor shall use his best endeavours:-

(i) to salve the ".."and/or her cargo freight bunkers

\# See Note 3 above

stores and any other property thereon and take them to #.. or
to such other place as may hereafter be agreed either place to be deemed a place of safety or if no such
place is named or agreed to a place of safety and
(ii) while performing the salvage services to prevent or minimize damage to the environment.

(b) Subject to the statutory provisions relating to special compensation the services shall be rendered and
accepted as salvage services upon the principle of "no cure - no pay."

(c) The Contractor's remuneration shall be fixed by Arbitration in London in the manner hereinafter
prescribed and any other difference arising out of this Agreement or the operations thereunder shall be
referred to Arbitration in the same way.

(d) In the event of the services referred to in this Agreement or any part of such services having been
already rendered at the date of this Agreement by the Contractor to the said vessel and/or her cargo
freight bunkers stores and any other property thereon the provisions of this Agreement shall apply to
such services.

\# See Note 3 above

(e) The security to be provided to the Council of Lloyd's (hereinafter called "the Council") the Salved
Value(s) the Award and/or any Interim Award(s) and/or any Award on Appeal shall be in
#... currency.

(f) If clause 1(e) is not completed then the security to be provided and the Salved Value(s) the Award
and/or Interim Award(s) and/or Award on Appeal shall be in Pounds Sterling.

(g) This Agreement and Arbitration thereunder shall except as otherwise expressly provided be governed
by the law of England, including the English law of salvage.

15.1 00
3.12.24
13.10.26
12.4.50
10.6.53
20.12.67
23.3.72
21.5.80
5.9.90
1.1.95

PROVISIONS AS TO THE SERVICES

2. *Definitions*: In this Agreement any reference to "Convention" is a reference to the International Convention on Salvage 1989 as incorporated in the Merchant Shipping (Salvage and Pollution) Act 1994 (and any amendment thereto). The terms "Contractor" and "services"/"salvage services" in this Agreement shall have the same meanings as the terms "salvor(s)" and "salvage operation(s)" in the Convention.

3. *Owners Cooperation*: The Owners their Servants and Agents shall co-operate fully with the Contractor in and about the salvage including obtaining entry to the place named or the place of safety as defined in clause 1. The Contractor may make reasonable use of the vessel's machinery gear equipment anchors chains stores and other appurtenances during and for the purpose of the salvage services free of expense but shall not unnecessarily damage abandon or sacrifice the same or any property the subject of this Agreement.

4. *Vessel Owners Right to Terminate*: When there is no longer any reasonable prospect of a useful result leading to a salvage reward in accordance with Convention Article 13 the owners of the vessel shall be entitled to terminate the services of the Contractor by giving reasonable notice to the Contractor in writing.

PROVISIONS AS TO SECURITY

5. (a) The Contractor shall immediately after the termination of the services or sooner notify the Council and where practicable the Owners of the amount for which he demands salvage security (inclusive of costs expenses and interest) from each of the respective Owners.

(b) Where a claim is made or may be made for special compensation, the owners of the vessel shall on the demand of the Contractor whenever made provide security for the Contractor's claim for special compensation provided always that such demand is made within two years of the date of termination of the services.

(c) The amount of any such security shall be reasonable in the light of the knowledge available to the Contractor at the time when the demand is made. Unless otherwise agreed such security shall be provided (i) to the Council (ii) in a form approved by the Council and (iii) by persons firms or corporations either acceptable to the Contractor or resident in the United Kingdom and acceptable to the Council. The Council shall not be responsible for the sufficiency (whether in amount or otherwise) of any security which shall be provided nor the default or insolvency of any person firm or corporation providing the same.

(d) The owners of the vessel their Servants and Agents shall use their best endeavours to ensure that the cargo owners provide their proportion of salvage security before the cargo is released.

6. (a) Until security has been provided as aforesaid the Contractor shall have a maritime lien on the property salved for his remuneration.

(b) The property salved shall not without the consent in writing of the Contractor (which shall not be unreasonably withheld) be removed from the place to which it has been taken by the Contractor under clause 1(a). Where such consent is given by the Contractor on condition that the Contractor is provided with temporary security pending completion of the voyage the Contractor's maritime lien on the property salved shall remain in force to the extent necessary to enable the Contractor to compel the provision of security in accordance with clause 5(c).

(c) The Contractor shall not arrest or detain the property salved unless:-

    (i) security is not provided within 14 days (exclusive of Saturdays and Sundays or other days observed as general holidays at Lloyd's) after the date of the termination of the services or

    (ii) he has reason to believe that the removal of the property salved is contemplated contrary to clause 6(b) or

    (iii) any attempt is made to remove the property salved contrary to clause 6(b).

(d) The Arbitrator appointed under clause 7 or the Appeal Arbitrator(s) appointed under clause 13(d) shall have power in their absolute discretion to include in the amount awarded to the Contractor the whole or part of any expenses reasonably incurred by the Contractor in:-

    (i) ascertaining demanding and obtaining the amount of security reasonably required in accordance with clause 5.

    (ii) enforcing and/or protecting by insurance or otherwise or taking reasonable steps to enforce and/or protect his lien.

PROVISIONS AS TO ARBITRATION

7.   (a) Whether security has been provided or not the Council shall appoint an Arbitrator upon receipt of a written request made by letter telex facsimile or in any other permanent form provided that any party requesting such appointment shall if required by the Council undertake to pay the reasonable fees and expenses of the Council and/or any Arbitrator or Appeal Arbitrator(s).

(b) Where an Arbitrator has been appointed and the parties do not proceed to arbitration the Council may recover any fees costs and/or expenses which are outstanding.

8.   The Contractor's remuneration and/or special compensation shall be fixed by the Arbitrator appointed under clause 7. Such remuneration shall not be diminished by reason of the exception to the principle of "no cure - no pay" in the form of special compensation.

REPRESENTATION

9.   Any party to this Agreement who wishes to be heard or to adduce evidence shall nominate a person in the United Kingdom to represent him failing which the Arbitrator or Appeal Arbitrator(s) may proceed as if such party had renounced his right to be heard or adduce evidence.

CONDUCT OF THE ARBITRATION

10.   (a) The Arbitrator shall have power to:-

- (i)   admit such oral or documentary evidence or information as he may think fit
- (ii) conduct the Arbitration in such manner in all respects as he may think fit subject to such procedural rules as the Council may approve
- (iii) order the Contractor in his absolute discretion to pay the whole or part of the expense of providing excessive security or security which has been unreasonably demanded under Clause 5(b) and to deduct such sum from the remuneration and/or special compensation
- (iv) make Interim Award(s) including payment(s) on account on such terms as may be fair and just
- (v)   make such orders as to costs fees and expenses including those of the Council charged under clauses 10(b) and 14(b) as may be fair and just.

(b) The Arbitrator and the Council may charge reasonable fees and expenses for their services whether the Arbitration proceeds to a hearing or not and all such fees and expenses shall be treated as part of the costs of the Arbitration.

(c) Any Award shall (subject to Appeal as provided in this Agreement) be final and binding on all the parties concerned whether they were represented at the Arbitration or not.

INTEREST & RATES OF EXCHANGE

11. *Interest*: Interest at rates per annum to be fixed by the Arbitrator shall (subject to Appeal as provided in this Agreement) be payable on any sum awarded taking into account any sums already paid:-

- (i)   from the date of termination of the services unless the Arbitrator shall in his absolute discretion otherwise decide until the date of publication by the Council of the Award and/or Interim Award(s) and
- (ii)   from the expiration of 21 days (exclusive of Saturdays and Sundays or other days observed as general holidays at Lloyd's) after the date of publication by the Council of the Award and/or Interim Award(s) until the date payment is received by the Contractor or the Council both dates inclusive.

For the purpose of sub-clause (ii) the expression "sum awarded" shall include the fees and expenses referred to in clause 10(b).

12. *Currency Correction*: In considering what sums of money have been expended by the Contractor in rendering the services and/or in fixing the amount of the Award and/or Interim Award(s) and/or Award on Appeal the Arbitrator or Appeal Arbitrator(s) shall to such an extent and in so far as it may be fair and just in all the circumstances give effect to the consequences of any change or changes in the relevant rates of exchange which may have occurred between the date of termination of the services and the date on which the Award and/or Interim Award(s) and/or Award on Appeal is made.

PROVISIONS AS TO APPEAL

13. (a) Notice of Appeal if any shall be given to the Council within 14 days (exclusive of Saturdays and Sundays or other days observed as general holidays at Lloyd's) after the date of the publication by the Council of the Award and/or Interim Award(s).

(b) Notice of Cross-Appeal if any shall be given to the Council within 14 days (exclusive of Saturdays and Sundays or other days observed as general holidays at Lloyd's) after notification by the Council to the parties of any Notice of Appeal. Such notification if sent by post shall be deemed received on the working day following the day of posting.

(c) Notice of Appeal or Cross-Appeal shall be given to the Council by letter telex facsimile or in any other permanent form.

(d) Upon receipt of Notice of Appeal the Council shall refer the Appeal to the hearing and determination of the Appeal Arbitrator(s) selected by it.

(e) If any Notice of Appeal or Cross-Appeal is withdrawn the Appeal hearing shall nevertheless proceed in respect of such Notice of Appeal or Cross-Appeal as may remain.

(f) Any Award on Appeal shall be final and binding on all the parties to that Appeal Arbitration whether they were represented either at the Arbitration or at the Appeal Arbitration or not.

CONDUCT OF THE APPEAL

14. (a) The Appeal Arbitrator(s) in addition to the powers of the Arbitrator under clauses 10(a) and 11 shall have power to:-

(i) admit the evidence which was before the Arbitrator together with the Arbitrator's notes and reasons for his Award and/or Interim Award(s) and any transcript of evidence and such additional evidence as he or they may think fit.

(ii) confirm increase or reduce the sum awarded by the Arbitrator and to make such order as to the payment of interest on such sum as he or they may think fit.

(iii) confirm revoke or vary any order and/or Declaratory Award made by the Arbitrator.

(iv) award interest on any fees and expenses charged under paragraph (b) of this clause from the expiration of 21 days (exclusive of Saturdays and Sundays or other days observed as general holidays at Lloyd's) after the date of publication by the Council of the Award on Appeal and/or Interim Award(s) on Appeal until the date payment is received by the Council both dates inclusive.

(b) The Appeal Arbitrator(s) and the Council may charge reasonable fees and expenses for their services in connection with the Appeal Arbitration whether it proceeds to a hearing or not and all such fees and expenses shall be treated as part of the costs of the Appeal Arbitration.

PROVISIONS AS TO PAYMENT

15. (a) In case of Arbitration if no Notice of Appeal be received by the Council in accordance with clause 13(a) the Council shall call upon the party or parties concerned to pay the amount awarded and in the event of non-payment shall subject to the Contractor first providing to the Council a satisfactory Undertaking to pay all the costs thereof realize or enforce the security and pay therefrom to the Contractor (whose receipt shall be a good discharge to it) the amount awarded to him together with interest if any. The Contractor shall reimburse the parties concerned to such extent as the Award is less than any sums paid on account or in respect of Interim Award(s).

(b) If Notice of Appeal be received by the Council in accordance with clause 13 it shall as soon as the Award on Appeal has been published by it call upon the party or parties concerned to pay the amount awarded and in the event of non-payment shall subject to the Contractor first providing to the Council a satisfactory Undertaking to pay all the costs thereof realize or enforce the security and pay therefrom to the Contractor (whose receipt shall be a good discharge to it) the amount awarded to him together with interest if any. The Contractor shall reimburse the parties concerned to such extent as the Award on Appeal is less than any sums paid on account or in respect of the Award or Interim Award(s).

(c) If any sum shall become payable to the Contractor as remuneration for his services and/or interest and/or costs as the result of an agreement made between the Contractor and the Owners or any of them the Council in the event of non-payment shall subject to the Contractor first providing to the Council a satisfactory Undertaking to pay all the costs thereof realize or enforce the security and pay therefrom to the Contractor (whose receipt shall be a good discharge to it) the said sum.

(d) If the Award and/or Interim Award(s) and/or Award on Appeal provides or provide that the costs of the Arbitration and/or of the Appeal Arbitration or any part of such costs shall be borne by the Contractor such costs may be deducted from the amount awarded or agreed before payment is made to the Contractor unless satisfactory security is provided by the Contractor for the payment of such costs.

(e) Without prejudice to the provisions of clause 5(c) the liability of the Council shall be limited in any event to the amount of security provided to it.

GENERAL PROVISIONS

16. *Scope of Authority*: The Master or other person signing this Agreement on behalf of the property to be salved enters into this Agreement as agent for the vessel her cargo freight bunkers stores and any other property thereon and the respective Owners thereof and binds each (but not the one for the other or himself personally) to the due performance thereof.

17. *Notices*: Any Award notice authority order or other document signed by the Chairman of Lloyd's or any person authorised by the Council for the purpose shall be deemed to have been duly made or given by the Council and shall have the same force and effect in all respects as if it had been signed by every member of the Council.

18. *Sub-Contractor(s)*: The Contractor may claim salvage and enforce any Award or agreement made between the Contractor and the Owners against security provided under clause 5 or otherwise if any on behalf of any Sub-Contractors his or their Servants or Agents including Masters and members of the crews of vessels employed by him or by any Sub-Contractors in the services provided that he first provides a reasonably satisfactory indemnity to the Owners against all claims by or liabilities to the said persons.

19. *Inducements prohibited*: No person signing this Agreement or any party on whose behalf it is signed shall at any time or in any manner whatsoever offer provide make give or promise to provide demand or take any form of inducement for entering into this Agreement.

For and on behalf of the Contractor	For and on behalf of the Owners of property to be salved.
.... (To be signed by the Contractor personally or by the Master of the salving vessel or other person whose name is inserted in line 4 of this Agreement)	.... (To be signed by the Master or other person whose name is inserted in line 1 of this Agreement)

INTERNATIONAL CONVENTION ON SALVAGE 1989

The following provisions of the Convention are set out below for information only.

Article 1

Definitions

(a) *Salvage operation* means any act or activity undertaken to assist a vessel or any other property in danger in navigable waters or in any other waters whatsoever

(b) *Vessel* means any ship or craft, or any structure capable of navigation

(c) *Property* means any property not permanently and intentionally attached to the shoreline and includes freight at risk

(d) *Damage to the environment* means substantial physical damage to human health or to marine life or resources in coastal or inland waters or areas adjacent thereto, caused by pollution, contamination, fire, explosion or similar major incidents

(e) *Payment* means any reward, remuneration or compensation due under this Convention

Article 6

Salvage Contracts

1.   This Convention shall apply to any salvage operations save to the extent that a contract otherwise provides expressly or by implication

2.   The master shall have the authority to conclude contracts for salvage operations on behalf of the owner of the vessel. The master or the owner of the vessel shall have the authority to conclude such contracts on behalf of the owner of the property on board the vessel

Article 8

Duties of the Salvor and of the Owner and Master

1.   The salvor shall owe a duty to the owner of the vessel or other property in danger:

   (a)   to carry out the salvage operations with due care;
   (b)   in performing the duty specified in subparagraph (a), to exercise due care to prevent or minimize damage to the environment;
   (c)   whenever circumstances reasonably require, to seek assistance from other salvors; and
   (d)   to accept the intervention of other salvors when reasonably requested to do so by the owner or master of the vessel or other property in danger; provided however that the amount of his reward shall not be prejudiced should it be found that such a request was unreasonable

2.   The owner and master of the vessel or the owner of other property in danger shall owe a duty to the salvor:

   (a)   to co-operate fully with him during the course of the salvage operations;
   (b)   in so doing, to exercise due care to prevent or minimize damage to the environment; and
   (c)   when the vessel or other property has been brought to a place of safety, to accept redelivery when reasonably requested by the salvor to do so

Article 13

Criteria for fixing the reward

1.   The reward shall be fixed with a view to encouraging salvage operations, taking into account the following criteria without regard to the order in which they are presented below:

   (a)   the salved value of the vessel and other property;
   (b)   the skill and efforts of the salvors in preventing or minimizing damage to the environment;
   (c)   the measure of success obtained by the salvor;
   (d)   the nature and degree of the danger;
   (e)   the skill and efforts of the salvors in salving the vessel, other property and life;
   (f)   the time used and expenses and losses incurred by the salvors;
   (g)   the risk of liability and other risks run by the salvors or their equipment;
   (h)   the promptness of the services rendered;
   (i)   the availability and use of vessels or other equipment intended for salvage operations;
   (j)   the state of readiness and efficiency of the salvor's equipment and the value thereof

2.   Payment of a reward fixed according to paragraph 1 shall be made by all of the vessel and other property interests in proportion to their respective salved values

3.   The rewards, exclusive of any interest and recoverable legal costs that may be payable thereon, shall not exceed the salved value of the vessel and other property

Article 14

Special Compensation

1.   If the salvor has carried out salvage operations in respect of a vessel which by itself or its cargo threatened damage to the environment and has failed to earn a reward under Article 13 at least equivalent to the special compensation assessable in accordance with this Article, he shall be entitled to special compensation from the owner of that vessel equivalent to his expenses as herein defined

2.   If, in the circumstances set out in paragraph 1, the salvor by his salvage operations has prevented or minimized damage to the environment, the special compensation payable by the owner to the salvor under paragraph 1 may be increased up to a maximum of 30% of the expenses incurred by the salvor. However, the Tribunal, if it deems it fair and just to do so and bearing in mind the relevant criteria set out in Article 13, paragraph 1, may increase such special compensation further, but in no event shall the total increase be more than 100% of the expenses incurred by the salvor

3.   Salvor's expenses for the purpose of paragraphs 1 and 2 means the out-of-pocket expenses reasonably incurred by the salvor in the salvage operation and a fair rate for equipment and personnel actually and reasonably used in the salvage operation, taking into consideration the criteria set out in Article 13, paragraph 1(h), (i) and (j)

4.   The total special compensation under this Article shall be paid only if and to the extent that such compensation is greater than any reward recoverable by the salvor under Article 13

5.   If the salvor has been negligent and has thereby failed to prevent or minimize damage to the environment, he may be deprived of the whole or part of any special compensation due under this Article

6.   Nothing in this Article shall affect any right of recourse on the part of the owner of the vessel

REVISION OF THE BILLS OF LADING ACT 1855—CARRIAGE OF GOODS BY SEA ACT 1992

A conflict having been identified in the cases of *The Delfini* [1990] 1 Lloyd's Rep. 252 and *The Aramis* [1989] 1 Lloyd's Rep. 213 between the 1855 Bills of Lading Act and the Sale of Goods Act, it became necessary as a matter of some urgency to resolve it, because it might otherwise affect the standing of London as a forum for arbitration. Briefly the conflict arose because the Sale of Goods Act provided that, in the case of sale of part of a homogeneous parcel of goods, title could not be claimed until the parcel to be sold be ascertained. Put more simply, if you buy 1,000 tons of grain out of a cargo of 4,000 tons in bulk in a hold, even though you have paid for it you cannot claim title to your 1,000 tons until it is separated from the other 3,000 tons.

This conflicted with the Bills of Lading Act provision:

"Every consignee of goods named in a bill of lading, and every indorsee of a bill of lading to whom property in the goods therein mentioned shall pass, upon or by reason of such consignment or indorsement, shall have transferred to and vested in him all rights of suit, and be subject to the same liabilities in respect of such goods as if the contract contained in the bill of lading has been made with himself."

which was designed to give a consignee under a bill of lading title to sue the carrier in his own name. However, because of the Sale of Goods Act, "property did not pass upon or by reason of such consignment or indorsement", so the consignee lost his right of suit against the carrier. Resuming the example above, if, when delivered, the 1,000 tons of grain was damaged, the consignee could not sue the carrier as he had no title at the time that the damage occurred.

The Law Commission produced a report entitled *Rights of Suit in Respect of Carriage of Goods by Sea* in March 1991 and this became law in the UK on 16 September 1992 as the Carriage of Goods by Sea Act 1992. It redressed the problem outlined above and took the opportunity to introduce some other updating of a non-contentious nature by being the first legislation to mention waybills and to provide for amendment to facilitate EDI. In relation to waybills, section 3(1) of the Act provides for consignees under waybills to enjoy the same rights against the carrier (and incur the same liabilities) when they "take or demand delivery or make a claim" as they would have as the holder of a bill of lading. The Act also provides in section 1(5) for the Secretary of

State to amend the Act to facilitate developments in information technology.

THE CARRIAGE OF GOODS BY SEA ACT 1992

An Act to replace the Bills of Lading Act 1855 with new provision with respect to bills of lading and certain other shipping documents.   [16th July 1992]

Shipping documents etc. to which act applies

1.—(1) This Act applies to the following documents, that is to say—
  (a) any bill of lading;
  (b) any sea waybill; and
  (c) any ship's delivery order.
 (2) References in this Act to a bill of lading—
  (a) do not include references to a document which is incapable of transfer either by indorsement or, as a bearer bill, by delivery without indorsement; but
  (b) subject to that, do include references to a received for shipment bill of lading.
 (3) References in this Act to a sea waybill are references to any document which is not a bill of lading but—
  (a) is such a receipt for goods as contains or evidences a contract for the carriage of goods by sea; and
  (b) identifies the person to whom delivery of the goods is to be made by the carrier in accordance with that contract.
 (4) References in this Act to a ship's delivery order are references to any document which is neither a bill of lading nor a sea waybill but contains an undertaking which—
  (a) is given under or for the purposes of a contract for the carriage by sea of the goods to which the document relates, or of goods which include those goods; and
  (b) is an undertaking by the carrier to a person identified in the document to deliver the goods to which the document relates to that person.
 (5) The Secretary of State may by regulations make provision for the application of this Act to cases where a telecommunication system or any other information technology is used for effecting transactions corresponding to—
  (a) the issue of a document to which this Act applies;
  (b) the indorsement, delivery or other transfer of such a document; or
  (c) the doing of anything else in relation to such a document.

(6) Regulations under subsection (5) above may—

    (*a*) make such modifications of the following provisions of this Act as the Secretary of State considers appropriate in connection with the application of this Act to any case mentioned in that subsection; and

    (*b*) contain supplemental, incidental, consequential and transitional provision;

and the power to make regulations under that subsection shall be exercisable by statutory instrument subject to annulment in pursuance of a resolution of either House of Parliament.

Rights under shipping documents

2.—(1) Subject to the following provisions of this section, a person who becomes—

    (*a*) the lawful holder of a bill of lading;

    (*b*) the person who (without being an original party to the contract of carriage) is the person to whom delivery of the goods to which a sea waybill relates is to be made by the carrier in accordance with that contract; or

    (*c*) the person to whom delivery of the goods to which a ship's delivery order relates is to be made in accordance with the undertaking contained in the order,

shall (by virtue of becoming the holder of the bill or, as the case may be, the person to whom delivery is to be made) have transferred to and vested in him all rights of suit under the contract of carriage as if he had been a party to that contract.

(2) Where, when a person becomes the lawful holder of a bill of lading, possession of the bill no longer gives a right (as against the carrier) to possession of the goods to which the bill relates, that person shall not have any rights transferred to him by virtue of subsection (1) above unless he becomes the holder of the bill—

    (*a*) by virtue of a transaction effected in pursuance of any contractual or other arrangements made before the time when such a right to possession ceased to attach to possession of the bill; or

    (*b*) as a result of the rejection to that person by another person of goods or documents delivered to the other person in pursuance of any such arrangements.

(3) The rights vested in any person by virtue of the operation of subsection (1) above in relation to a ship's delivery order—

    (*a*) shall be so vested subject to the terms of the order; and

    (*b*) where the goods to which the order relates form a part only of the goods to which the contract of carriage relates, shall be confined to rights in respect of the goods to which the order relates.

(4) Where, in the case of any documents to which this Act applies—

- (a) a person with any interest or right in or in relation to goods to which the document relates sustains loss or damage in consequence of a breach of the contract of carriage; but
- (b) subsection (1) above operates in relation to that document so that rights of suit in respect of that breach are vested in another person,

the other person shall be entitled to exercise those rights for the benefit of the person who sustained the loss or damage to the same extent as they could have been exercised if they had been vested in the person for whose benefit they are exercised.

(5) Where rights are transferred by virtue of the operation of subsection (1) above in relation to any document, the transfer for which that subsection provides shall extinguish any entitlement to those rights which derives—

- (a) where that document is a bill of lading, from a person's having been an original party to the contract of carriage; or
- (b) in the case of any document to which this Act applies, from the previous operation of that subsection in relation to that document;

but the operation of that subsection shall be without prejudice to any rights which derive from a person's having been an original party to the contract contained in, or evidenced by, a sea waybill and, in relation to a ship's delivery order, shall be without prejudice to any rights deriving otherwise than from the previous operation of that subsection in relation to that order.

Liabilities under shipping documents

3.—(1) Where subsection (1) of section 2 of this Act operates in relation to any document to which this Act applies and the person in whom rights are vested by virtue of that subsection—

- (a) takes or demands delivery from the carrier of any of the goods to which the document relates;
- (b) makes a claim under the contract of carriage against the carrier in respect of any of those goods; or
- (c) is a person who, at a time before those rights were vested in him, took or demanded delivery from the carrier of any of those goods,

that person shall (by virtue of taking or demanding delivery or making the claim or, in a case falling within paragraph (c) above, of having the rights vested in him) become subject to the same liabilities under that contract as if he had been a party to that contract.

(2) Where the goods to which a ship's delivery order relates form a part only of the goods to which the contract of carriage relates, the liabilities to which any person is subject by virtue of the operation of this section in relation to that order shall exclude liabilities in respect of any goods to which the order does not relate.

(3) This section, so far as it imposes liabilities under any contract on any person, shall be without prejudice to the liabilities under the contract of any person as an original party to the contract.

Representations in bills of lading

4. A bill of lading which—
- (a) represents goods to have been shipped on board a vessel or to have been received for shipment on board a vessel; and
- (b) has been signed by the master of the vessel or by a person who was not the master but had the express, implied or apparent authority of the carrier to sign bills of lading,

shall, in favour of a person who has become the lawful holder of the bill, be conclusive evidence against the carrier of the shipment of the goods or, as the case may be, of their receipt for shipment.

Interpretation etc.

5.—(1) In this Act—
"bill of lading", "sea waybill" and "ship's delivery order" shall be construed in accordance with section 1 above;
"the contract of carriage"—
(a) in relation to a bill of lading or sea waybill, means the contract contained in or evidenced by that bill or waybill; and
(b) in relation to a ship's delivery order, means the contract under or for the purposes of which the undertaking contained in the order is given;
"holder", in relation to a bill of lading, shall be construed in accordance with subsection (2) below;
"information technology" includes any computer or other technology by means of which information or other matter may be recorded or communicated without being reduced to documentary form; and
"telecommunication system" has the same meaning as in the Telecommunications Act 1984.

(2) References to this Act to the holder of a bill of lading are references to any of the following persons, that is to say—
- (a) a person with possession of the bill who, by virtue of being the person identified in the bill, is the consignee of the goods to which the bill relates;
- (b) a person with possession of the bill as a result of the completion, by delivery of the bill, of any indorsement of the bill or, in the case of a bearer bill, or any other transfer of the bill;
- (c) a person with possession of the bill as a result of any transaction by virtue of which he would have become a holder (falling within paragraph (a) or (b) above had not the transaction been effected at

a time when possession of the bill no longer gave a right (as against the carrier) to possession of the goods to which the bill relates; and a person shall be regarded for the purposes of this Act as having become the lawful holder of a bill of lading wherever he has become the holder of the bill in good faith.

(3) References in this Act to a person's being identified in a document include references to his being identified by a description which allows for the identity of the person in question to be varied, in accordance with the terms of the document, after its issue; and the reference in section 1(3)(*b*) of this Act to a document's identifying a person shall be construed accordingly.

(4) Without prejudice to sections 2(2) and 4 above, nothing in this Act shall preclude its operation in relation to a case where the goods to which a document relates—

    (*a*) cease to exist after the issue of the document; or

    (*b*) cannot be identified (whether because they are mixed with other goods or for any other reason);

and references in this Act to the goods to which a document relates shall be construed accordingly.

(5) The preceding provisions of this Act shall have effect without prejudice to the application, in relation to any case, of the rules (the Hague-Visby Rules) which for the time being have the force of law by virtue of section 1 of the Carriage of Goods by Sea Act 1971.

Short title, repeal, commencement and extent

6.—(1) This Act may be cited as the Carriage of Goods by Sea Act 1992.

(2) The Bills of Lading Act 1855 is hereby repealed.

(3) This Act shall come into force at the end of the period of two months beginning with the day on which it is passed; but nothing in this Act shall have effect in relation to any document issued before the coming into force of this Act.

(4) This Act extends to Northern Ireland.

PROPOSED AMENDMENTS TO THE CARRIAGE OF GOODS BY SEA ACT 1936 (US)

THE PROPOSED BILL

THE CARRIAGE OF GOODS BY SEA BILL

An Act to amend the Carriage of Goods by Sea Act, and for other purposes

Be it enacted by the Senate and House of Representatives of the United States of America in Congress assembled, That the Carriage of Goods by Sea Act of 1936, 46 U.S.C. App. §§ 1300–1315, is hereby amended to read as follows:

Enacting Clause, 46 U.S.C. App. § 1300

Be it enacted by the Senate and House of Representatives of the United States of America in Congress assembled, That every contract that includes the carriage of goods by sea covering transportation to or from the United States shall have effect subject to the provisions of this Act. The defenses and limitations of liability provided for in this Act and the responsibilities imposed by this Act shall apply with the force of law in any action against a carrier or a ship in respect of loss or damage to goods covered by a contract of carriage without regard for the form or theory of the action or the court or other tribunal in which it is brought. The remedies available under this Act shall constitute the complete and exclusive remedy against a carrier in respect of loss or damage to goods covered by a contract of carriage. This Act shall be construed as providing an independent basis for admiralty jurisdiction.

Section 1, 46 U.S.C. App. § 1301

When used in this Act—
(a) (i) The term "carrier" includes contracting carriers, performing carriers, and ocean carriers.

135

    (ii) The term "contracting carrier" means the party who enters into the contract of carriage with the shipper of the goods.

    (iii) The term "performing carrier" means a party who performs or undertakes to perform any of the contracting carrier's responsibilities under a contract of carriage, including any party that performs or undertakes to perform or procures to be performed any incidental service to facilitate the carriage of goods, regardless of whether it is a party to, identified in, or has legal responsibility under the contract of carriage. The term includes, but is not limited to, ocean carriers, inland carriers, stevedores, terminal operators, consolidators, packers, warehousemen, and their servants, agents, contractors, and sub-contractors. A contracting carrier may also be a performing carrier.

    (iv) The term "ocean carrier" means a performing carrier who owns, operates, or charters a ship used in the carriage of the goods by sea,

    (iv) This Act shall not apply to claims against an interstate motor or rail carrier that is not the contracting carrier to the extent that it is providing motor or rail services.

(b) The term "contract of carriage" applies to all contracts for the carriage of goods either by sea or partially by sea and partially by one or more other modes of transportation, but does not include (i) contracts for transportation in domestic trade exclusively on the Great Lakes, rivers or other inland waters, or the intercoastal waterway, or (ii) charterparties. The term "contract of carriage" includes, but is not limited to, negotiable or "order" bills of lading and non-negotiable or "straight" bills of lading, whether printed or electronic. Any bill of lading or other contract arising under or pursuant to a charterparty shall be included in the term "contract of carriage" from the moment at which it regulates the relations between a carrier and a holder of the same.

(c) The term "goods" includes goods, wares, merchandise, and articles of every kind whatsoever, except live animals.

(d) The term "ship" means any vessel used for the carriage of goods by sea.

(e) The term "carriage of goods" covers the period from the time the goods are received by a carrier to the time they are delivered by a carrier to a person authorized to receive them.

(f) The term "shipper" means any person by whom or in whose name or on whose behalf a contract of carriage has been concluded with a contracting carrier, or any person by whom or in whose name or on whose behalf the goods are actually delivered to a carrier in relation to the contract of carriage.

(g) In this Act, the term "electronic" shall include Electronic Data Interchange (EDI) or other computerized media. If the parties agree to use an electronic bill of lading, it shall be a "contract of carriage" governed by this Act and the procedures for such bills of lading shall be in accordance with rules agreed upon by the parties.

Section 2, 46 U.S.C. App. § 1302

Subject to the provisions of section 6, under every contract of carriage, the carriers in relation to the receiving loading, handling, stowage, carriage, custody, care, discharge, and delivery of the goods, shall be subject to the responsibilities and liabilities and entitled to the rights and immunities hereinafter set forth. A contracting carrier shall be subject to these responsibilities and liabilities and entitled to these rights and immunities with respect to the entire period covered by its contract of carriage. A performing carrier shall be subject to these responsibilities and liabilities and entitled to these rights and immunities (i) during the period between the time it has received the goods or taken them in charge and the time it has relinquished control of the goods pursuant to the contract of carriage and (ii) at any other time to the extent that it is participating in the performance of any of the activities contemplated by the contract of carriage.

Section 3, 46 U.S.C. App. § 1303

(1) The contracting and ocean carriers shall be bound, before and at the beginning of the voyage, to exercise due diligence to—
   (*a*) Make the ship seaworthy;
   (*b*) Properly man, equip, and supply the ship;
   (*c*) Make the holds, refrigerating and cooling chambers, and all other parts of the ship in which goods are carried, fit and safe for their reception, carriage, and preservation.
(2) The carriers shall properly and carefully receive, load, handle, stow, carry, keep, care for, discharge, and deliver the goods carried.
(3) (i) After a carrier receives the goods into its charge, the contracting carrier shall, on demand of the shipper, issue to the shipper a negotiable bill of lading or, if the shipper agrees, a non-negotiable bill of lading. This contract of carriage shall show, among other things—
      (*a*) The leading marks necessary for identification of the goods as the same are furnished in writing by the shipper before a carrier receives the goods, provided such marks are stamped or otherwise shown clearly upon the goods if uncovered, or on the cases or coverings in which such goods are contained, in such a manner as should ordinarily remain legible until the end of the voyage;

(b) Either the number of packages or pieces, or the quantity or weight, as the case may be, as furnished in writing by the shipper; and

(c) The apparent order and condition of the goods;

Provided, That the contracting carrier shall not be bound to state or show any marks, number, quantity, or weight information which a carrier has reasonable ground for suspecting not accurately to represent the goods actually received, or which a carrier has had no reasonable means of checking.

(ii) If a carrier issues a contract of carriage for non-containerized goods stating any marks, number, quantity, or weight information furnished by the shipper or its agents and a carrier can demonstrate that no carrier had a reasonable means of checking this information before the contract of carriage was issued, and the statement is qualified in a manner to indicate that no carrier has verified its accuracy (with a phrase such as "said to contain" or "shipper's weight, load, and count"), then a statement specifying any marks, number, quantity , or weight information in a contract of carriage that has been qualified as provided in this paragraph shall not constitute prima facie evidence that a carrier received the goods from the shipper as described in the contract of carriage, nor shall the qualified statement preclude any carrier from proving that no carrier received the goods from the shipper as described in the contract of carriage, unless the carrier was not entitled to qualify the statement under the requirements of this paragraph or a person relying on the statement in the contract of carriage proves that the contracting carrier was not acting in good faith when issuing the contract of carriage.

(iii) (a) If a carrier issues a contract of carriage stating any marks, number, or quantity information furnished by the shipper or its agents for goods shipped in a container loaded and sealed by the shipper or its agents, and a carrier can demonstrate that no carrier verified the container's contents before the contract of carriage was issued, then the carrier may qualify the statement in a manner to indicate that no carrier has verified its accuracy (with a phrase such as "said to contain" or "shipper's load, stow, and count"). If a carrier delivers the container intact and undamaged with the seal intact and undamaged, then a statement specifying any marks, number, or quantity in a contract of carriage that has been qualified as provided in this paragraph shall not constitute prima facie evidence that a carrier received the goods from the shipper as described in the contract of carriage, nor shall the qualified statement preclude any carrier from proving that no carrier received the goods from the shipper as described in the contract of carriage, unless the carrier was not entitled to qualify the statement under the requirements of this paragraph or a person relying on the statement in the contract of carriage proves that the contracting carrier was not acting in good faith when issuing the contract of carriage.

(b) If a carrier issues a contract of carriage stating the weight of goods shipped in a container loaded and sealed by the shipper or its agents, or the weight of the container including the goods, and a carrier can demonstrate that no carrier weighed the container before the contract of carriage was issued, then the carrier may qualify the statement of weight with an express statement that the container has not been weighed: *Provided,* That if the shipper and the contracting carrier agreed in writing before a carrier received the goods for shipment that a carrier would weigh the container, then the contracting carrier may not qualify the statement of weight. If a carrier delivers the container intact and undamaged with the seal intact and undamaged, then a statement of weight in a contract of carriage that has been qualified as provided in this paragraph shall not constitute prima facie evidence that a carrier received the goods from the shipper as described in the contract of carriage, nor shall the qualified statement preclude any carrier from proving that no carrier received the goods from the shipper as described in the contract of carriage, unless the carrier was not entitled to qualify the statement under the requirements of this paragraph or a person relying on the statement in the contract of carriage proves that the contracting carrier was not acting in good faith when, issuing the contract of carriage.

(4) (a) Except as provided in this section, a contract of carriage issued by or on behalf of a carrier shall be prima facie evidence of the receipt by that carrier of the goods as therein described.

(b) When this Act applies, the rules stated herein shall apply in lieu of inconsistent provisions of the Act, as amended, entitled "An Act relating to bills of lading in interstate and foreign commerce," approved August 29, 1916 (U.S.C., title 49, secs. 81–124), commonly known as the "Pomerene Bills of Lading Act," which is otherwise unaffected by this Act:

   (1) A contract of carriage in which it is stated that the goods are consigned or destined to a specified person is a non-negotiable or straight bill of lading. Sea waybills, express bills, and similar non-negotiable bills of lading are straight bills of lading for the purposes of this Act.

   (2) A contract of carriage in which it is stated that the goods are consigned or destined to the order of any person named in such contract of carriage is a negotiable or order bill of lading.

Any provision in a negotiable or order bill of lading or in any notice, contract, rule, regulation, or tariff that it is non-negotiable shall be null and void and shall not affect its negotiability within the meaning of this Act and the "Pomerene Bills of Lading Act" unless upon its face and in writing agreed to by the shipper. The insertion in a negotiable or order bill of lading of the name of a person to be notified of the arrival of the goods shall not limit the negotiability of the bill of lading or constitute notice to a purchaser thereof of any rights or equities of such person in the goods.

(3) A carrier, in the absence of some lawful excuse, is bound to deliver goods upon a demand made either by the consignee named in the contract of carriage for the goods or, if the contract of carriage is a negotiable or order bill of lading, by the holder thereof, if such a demand is accompanied by—

   (i) An offer in good faith to satisfy the carrier's lawful lien upon the goods;

   (ii) If the contract of carriage is a negotiable or order bill of lading, possession of the bill of lading and an offer in good faith to surrender, properly indorsed, the bill of lading which was issued for the goods; and

   (iii) A readiness and willingness to sign, when the goods are delivered, an acknowledgment that they have been delivered, if such signature is requested by the carrier.

In case the carrier refuses or fails to deliver the goods, in compliance with a demand by the consignee or holder so accompanied, the burden shall be upon the carrier to establish the existence of a lawful excuse for such refusal or failure.

(4) A carrier is justified, subject to the provisions of subsections 3(4)(b)(5), 3(4)(b)(6), and 3(4)(b)(7), in delivering goods to one who is—

   (i) A person lawfully entitled to the possession of the goods; or

   (ii) The consignee named in a non-negotiable or straight bill of lading for the goods, or

   (iii) A person in possession of a negotiable or order bill of lading for the goods by the terms of which the goods are deliverable to that person's order; or which has been indorsed to that person, or in blank by the consignee, or by the mediate or immediate indorsee of the consignee.

(5) If a carrier delivers goods to one who is not lawfully entitled to the possession of them, the carrier shall be liable to anyone having a right of property or possession in the goods if it delivered the goods otherwise than as authorized by subdivisions (ii) and (iii) of subsection 3(4)(b)(4); and, though the

carrier delivered the goods as authorized by either of said subdivisions. It shall be so liable if prior to such delivery it—

(i) Had been requested, by or on behalf of a person having a right of property or possession in the goods, not to make such delivery, or

(ii) Had information at the time of the delivery that it was to a person not lawfully entitled to the possession of the goods.

Such request or information, to be effective within the meaning of this paragraph, must be given to an officer or agent of the carrier, the actual or apparent scope of whose duties includes action upon such a request or information, and must be given in time to enable the officer or agent to whom it is given, acting with reasonable diligence, to stop delivery of the goods.

(6) Except as provided in paragraph (14) of this subsection, and except when compelled by legal process, if a carrier delivers goods for which a negotiable or order bill of lading had been issued, the negotiation of which would transfer the right to the possession of the goods, and fails to take up and cancel the bill of lading, such carrier shall be liable for failure to deliver the goods to anyone who for value and in good faith purchases such bill of lading, whether such purchaser acquired title to the bill of lading before or after the delivery of the goods by the carrier and notwithstanding delivery was made to the person entitled thereto.

(7) Except as provided in paragraph (14) of this subsection, and except when compelled by legal process, if a carrier delivers part of the goods for which a negotiable or order bill of lading had been issued and fails either—

(i) To take up and cancel the bill of lading, or

(ii) To place plainly upon it a statement that a portion of the goods has been delivered with a description which may be in general terms either of the goods or packages that have been so delivered or of the goods or packages which still remain in the carrier's possession,

the carrier shall be liable for failure to deliver all the goods specified in the bill of lading to anyone who for value and in good faith purchases it, whether such purchaser acquired title to it before or after the delivery of any portion of the goods by the carrier, and notwithstanding such delivery was made to the person entitled thereto.

(8) A contract of carriage shall describe the condition of the goods at the time a carrier received them from the shipper: *Provided,* that an "on-board" contract of carriage shall also describe the

condition of the goods at the time that they are loaded on board the ship or another mode of transportation. Any alteration, addition, or erasure in a contract of carriage after its issue without authority from the carrier issuing the same, either in writing or noted on the contract of carriage, shall be void, whatever be the nature and purpose of the change, and the contract of carriage shall be enforceable according to its original tenor.

(9) If a negotiable or order bill of lading has been lost, stolen, or destroyed, a court of competent jurisdiction may order the delivery of the goods upon satisfactory proof of such loss, theft, or destruction and upon the giving of a bond with sufficient surety, to be approved by the court, to protect the carrier or any person injured by such delivery from any liability or loss incurred by reason of the original bill of lading remaining outstanding. The court may also in its discretion order the payment of the carrier's reasonable costs and counsel fees: *Provided,* a voluntary indemnifying bond without order of court shall be binding on the parties thereto.

The delivery of the goods under the order of the court, as provided in this paragraph, shall not relieve the carrier from liability to a person to whom the negotiable or order bill of lading has been or shall be negotiated for value without notice of the proceedings or of the delivery of the goods.

(10) If more than one person claim the title or possession of goods, a carrier may require all known claimants to interplead, either as a defense to an action brought against the carrier for non-delivery of the goods or as an original suit, whichever is appropriate.

(11) If someone other than the consignee or the person in possession of the contract of carriage has a claim to the title or possession of the goods, and the carrier has information of such claim, the carrier shall be excused from liability for refusing to deliver the goods, either to the consignee or person in possession of the contract of carriage or to the adverse claimant, until the carrier has had a reasonable time to ascertain the validity of the adverse claim or to bring legal proceedings to compel all claimants to interplead.

(12) Except as provided in subsections 3(4)(*b*)(4), 3(4)(*b*)(10), and 3(4)(*b*)(11), no right or title of a third person, unless enforced by legal process, shall be a defense to an action brought by the consignee of a non-negotiable or straight bill of lading or by the holder of a negotiable or order bill of lading against the carrier for failure to delivery the goods on demand.

(13) If a contract of carriage has been issued by a contracting carrier or on its behalf by an agent or employee the scope of whose actual or apparent authority includes the receiving of goods and the issuing of contracts of carriage therefor, the carrier shall be liable to (a) the owner of goods covered by a non-negotiable or straight bill of lading subject to existing right of stoppage in transitu or (b) the holder of a negotiable or order bill of lading, who has given value in good faith, relying upon the description therein of the goods, or upon the shipment being made upon the date therein shown, for damages caused by the nonreceipt by the carrier of all or part of the goods upon or prior to the date therein shown, or their failure to correspond with the description thereof in the bill of lading at the time of its issue.

(14) If a negotiable or order bill of lading is issued, the carrier shall have a lien on the goods therein mentioned for all charges on those goods for freight, storage, demurrage and terminal charges, and expenses necessary for the preservation of the goods or incident to their transportation subsequent to the date of the bill of lading and all other charges incurred in transportation and delivery, unless the bill of lading expressly enumerates other charges for which a lien is claimed. In such case there shall also be a lien for the charges enumerated so far as they are allowed by law and the contract between the shipper and the carrier.

(15) After goods have been lawfully sold to satisfy a carrier's lien, or because they have not been claimed, or because they are perishable or hazardous, the carrier shall not, thereafter be liable for failure to deliver the goods themselves to the consignee or owner of the goods, or to a holder of the contract of carriage given for the goods when they were shipped, even if such contract of carriage be a negotiable or order bill of lading.

(5) The shipper shall be deemed to have guarantee to the carriers the accuracy at the time of shipment of the marks, number, quantity, and weight, as furnished by the shipper; and the shipper shall indemnify the carriers against all loss, damages, and expenses arising or resulting from inaccuracies in such particulars. The right of the carriers to such indemnity shall in no way limit their responsibility and liability under the contract of carriage to any person other than the shipper.

(6) (*a*) Unless notice of loss or damage and the general nature of such loss or damage be given in writing to the contracting carrier or the performing carrier making the delivery, or one of their agents, before or at the time of the delivery of the goods to the person entitled to receive them under the contract of carriage, such delivery shall be prima facie evidence of the delivery by the carriers of

the goods as described in the contract of carriage. If the loss or damage is not apparent, the notice must be given within three days of the delivery.

(*b*) Said notice of loss or damage may be endorsed upon the receipt for the goods given by the person taking delivery thereof.

(*c*) The notice in writing need not be given if the state of the goods has at the time of their receipt been the subject of joint survey or inspection.

(*d*) (i) In any event the carriers and their ships shall be discharged from all liability in respect of loss or damage unless suit is brought within one year after delivery of the goods or the date when the goods should have been delivered: *Provided,* That if a notice of loss or damage, either apparent or concealed, is not given as provided for in this section, that fact shall not affect or prejudice any party's right to bring suit within one year after the delivery of the goods or the date when the goods should have been delivered.

(ii) Notwithstanding the limitation period established in subsection 3(6)(*d*)(i), if a timely suit is brought against a carrier under this Act, that carrier shall have three months from the date when judgment is entered or a settlement is concluded to bring an action for contribution or indemnity against any other party in the transaction.

(iii) Notwithstanding the limitation period established in subsection 3(6)(*d*)(i), if the contract of carriage provides for arbitration, a claim shall be timely if a suit or an arbitration proceeding is commenced within one year after delivery of the goods or the date when the goods should have been delivered.

(*e*) in the case of any actual or apprehended loss or damage the carriers and the receiver shall give all reasonable facilities to each other for inspecting and tallying the goods, including joint surveys when appropriate.

(7) After the goods are loaded onto a ship or other mode of transportation the contract of carriage to be issued by the contracting carrier shall, if the shipper so demands, be a "shipped" contract of carriage: *Provided,* That if the shipper shall have previously taken up any contract of carriage for such goods, the shipper shall surrender the same as against the issue of the "shipped" contract of carriage, but at the option of the contracting carrier such contract of carriage may be noted at the port of shipment by the contracting carrier with the name or names of the ship or ships upon which the goods have been shipped and the date or dates of shipment, and when so noted the same shall for the purpose of this section be deemed to constitute a "shipped" contract of carriage.

(8) (*a*) Any clause, covenant, or agreement in a contract of carriage

relieving a carrier or a ship from liability for loss or damage to or in connection with the goods, arising from negligence, fault, or failure in the duties and obligations provided in this section, or lessening such liability otherwise than as provided in this Act, shall be null and void and of no effect: *Provident*, That this subsection shall not apply to a provision in a service contract, as defined in section 3(21) of the Shipping Act of 1984, to the extent that the provision affects only the rights and liabilities of the parties who entered into the service contract. A benefit of insurance in favor of a carrier, or similar clause, shall be deemed to be a clause relieving a carrier from liability.

(*b*) Any clause, covenant, or agreement made before a claim has arisen that specified a foreign forum for litigation or arbitration of a dispute governed by this Act shall be null and void and of no effect if:

　(i) the port of loading or the port of discharge is or was intended to be in the United States; or

　(ii) the place where the goods are received by a carrier or the place where the goods are delivered to a person authorized to receive them is or was intended to be in the United States;

provided, however, that if a clause, covenant, or agreement made before a claim has arisen specifies a foreign forum for arbitration of a dispute governed by this Act, then a court, on the timely motion of either party, shall order that arbitration shall proceed in the United States.

Section 4, 46 U.S.C. App. § 1304

(1) Neither a carrier nor a ship shall be liable for loss or damage arising or resulting from unseaworthiness unless caused by want of due diligence on the part of the carrier to make the ship seaworthy, and to secure that the ship is properly manned, equipped, and supplied, and to make the holds, refrigerating and cool chambers, and all other parts of the ship in which goods are carried fit and safe for their reception, carriage, and preservation in accordance with the provisions of subsection 3(1). Whenever loss or damage has resulted from unseaworthiness, the burden of proving the exercise of due diligence shall be on the carrier or other persons claiming exemption under this subsection.

(2) The carriers and their ships shall not be responsible for loss or damage arising or resulting from—

(*a*) [reserved]

(*b*) Fire on a ship, *provided, however*, that this exemption applies only for the benefit of (i) an ocean carrier, unless the fire was caused by its actual fault or privity, with respect to a fire on a ship that it furnished, and (ii) a contracting carrier, unless the fire was caused by its actual fault or privity.

(c) perils, dangers, and accidents of the sea or other navigable waters;

(d) Act of God;

(e) Act of war;

(f) Act of public enemies;

(g) Arrest or restraint of princes, rulers, or people, or seizure under legal process;

(h) Quarantine restrictions;

(i) Act or omission of the shipper or owner of the goods, its agent or representative;

(j) Strikes or lockouts or stoppage or restraint of labor from whatever cause, whether partial or general; *Provided,* that nothing herein contained shall be construed to relieve a carrier from responsibility for the carrier's own acts;

(k) Riots and civil commotions;

(l) Saving or attempting to save life or property at sea;

(m) Wastage in bulk or weight or any other loss or damage arising from inherent defect, quality, or vice of the goods;

(n) Insufficiency of packing;

(o) Insufficiency or inadequacy of marks;

(p) Latent defects not discoverable by due diligence; and

(q) Any other cause arising without the actual fault and privity of the carrier claiming the benefit of this exception and without the fault or neglect of its agents or servants, but the burden of proof shall be on that carrier to show that neither its actual fault or privity nor the fault or neglect of its agents or servants contributed to the loss or damage;

Provided, That if any person contends that the master, mariner, pilot, or servants of the ocean carrier were negligent in the navigation or management of the ship, the burden shall be on that person to prove negligence in the navigation or management of the ship; and *Provided further,* That where loss or damage is caused in part by a breach of a carrier's obligations or the fault or neglect of a carrier and in part by one or more of the excepted perils specified in this subsection, the carriers shall be liable for the loss or damage to the extent that it is attributable to such breach, fault, or neglect, and shall not be liable for the loss or damage to the extent that it is attributable to one or more of the excepted perils specified in this subsection. If there is no evidence to enable the trier of fact to determine the extent to which the loss or damage is attributable to such breach, fault, or neglect and the extent to which it is attributable to one or more of the excepted perils specified in this subsection, then the carriers shall be liable for one-half of the loss or damage.

(3) The shipper shall not be responsible for loss or damage sustained by a carrier or a ship arising or resulting from any cause without the act, fault, or neglect of the shipper, its agents, or its servants.

(4) Any deviation in saving or attempting to save life or property at sea, or any reasonable deviation shall not be deemed to be an infringement or breach of this Act or if the contract of carriage, and the carriers and their ships shall not be liable for any loss or damage resulting therefrom: *Provided, however,* That if the deviation is for the purpose of loading or unloading cargo or passengers it shall, prima facie, be regarded as unreasonable. An unreasonable deviation shall be considered a breach of the carriers' obligations under this Act, but the remedies available for the breach shall be governed by the provisions of this act, including subsections 4(2) and 4(5).

(5) (*a*) (1) Except as provided in subsection 4(5)(*b*) and subsection 4(5)(*e*), the aggregate liability of the carriers and their ships for any loss or damage to or in connection with the carriage of goods shall not under any circumstances exceed 666.67 Special Drawing Rights (as defined by the International Monetary Fund) per package, or two Special Drawing Rights per kilogram of gross weight of the goods lost or damaged, whichever is the higher.

(2) If a container, pallet, or similar article of transport is used to consolidate goods, the number of packages enumerated in the contract of carriage as packed in such article of transport shall be deemed the number of packages for the purpose of this section as far as these packages are concerned. Except as aforesaid, such article of transport shall be considered the package.

(*b*) (1) The limits mentioned in subsection 4(5)(*a*) shall not apply if the nature and value of the goods have been declared by the shipper before shipment and inserted in the contract of carriage. This declaration, if embodied in the contract of carriage, shall be prima facie evidence, but shall not be conclusive on a carrier.

(2) By agreement between the contracting carrier and the shipper different maximum amounts than those mentioned in subsection 4(5)(*a*) may be fixed: *Provided,* That such maximum amounts shall not be less than the figures above named except in a service contract, as defined in section 3(21) of the Shipping Act of 1984. Any agreement to alter the maximum amounts mentioned in subsection 4(5)(*a*) binds only the parties who entered into the agreement.

(*c*) In no event shall a carrier or a ship be liable for more than the amount of damage actually sustained.

(*d*) The carriers and their ships shall not be responsible in any event for loss or damage to or in connection with the carriage of goods if the nature or value thereof has been knowingly and fraudulently misstated by the shipper in the contract of carriage.

(*e*) A carrier shall not be entitled to the benefit of the limitation of liability provided for in subsection 4(5)(*a*) if it is proved that the loss or damage resulted (1) from an act or omission of that carrier, within the privity or knowledge of that carrier, done with the intent to cause such loss or damage, or recklessly and with knowledge that such loss or damage would probably result, or (2) from that carrier's unreasonable deviation which that carrier knew or should have known would result in such a loss or damage. One carrier's loss under this subsection of the benefit of the limitation of liability provided for in subsection 4(5)(*a*) shall not affect the right of any other carrier to claim that benefit.

(6) Goods of an inflammable, explosive, or dangerous nature to the shipment whereof the contracting carrier has not consented with knowledge of their nature and character, may at any time before discharge be landed at any place or destroyed or rendered innocuous by a carrier without compensation, and the shipper of such goods shall be liable for all damages and expenses directly or indirectly arising out of or resulting from such shipment. If any such goods shipped with such knowledge and consent shall become a danger to the ship or cargo, they may in like manner be landed at any place, or destroyed or rendered innocuous by a carrier without liability on the part of the carrier except to general average, if any.

Section 5, 46 U.S.C. App. § 1305

A contracting carrier shall be at liberty to surrender in whole or in part all or any of its rights and immunities or to increase any of its responsibilities and liabilities under this Act, provided such surrender or increase shall be embodied in the contract of carriage.

If a performing carrier's contract or tariff applies to the carriage of particular goods and provides for a higher level of responsibility or liability than that provided under this Act, then in an action against the performing carrier for loss or damage to those goods the claimant shall be entitled to the benefit of the higher level of responsibility or liability as provided in the performing carrier's contract or tariff.

Nothing in this Act shall be held to prevent the insertion in a contract of carriage of any lawful provision regarding general average.

Section 6, 46 U.S.C. App. § 1306

Notwithstanding the provisions of the preceding sections, a contracting carrier and a shipper shall, in regard to any particular goods be at liberty to enter into any agreement in any terms as to the responsibility and liability of the carriers for such goods, and as to the rights and immunities of the carriers in respect of such goods, or their obligations as to seaworthiness (so far as the stipulation regarding seaworthiness is not contrary to public policy), or the care or diligence of their servants or agents in regard to the receiving, loading, handling, stowage, carriage, custody, care, discharge, and delivery of the goods carried by sea: *Provided*, That in this case no bill of lading has been or shall be issued and that the terms agreed shall be embodied in a receipt which shall be a nonnegotiable document and shall be marked as such.

Any agreement so entered into shall have full legal effect: *Provided*, That this section shall not apply to ordinary commercial shipments made in the ordinary course of trade but only to other shipments where the character or condition of the property to be carried or the circumstances, terms, and conditions under which the carriage is to be performed are such as reasonably to justify a special agreement.

Section 8, 46 U.S.C. App. § 1308

The provisions of this Act shall not affect the rights and obligations of the carriers under the provisions of the Shipping Act, 1916, the Shipping Act of 1984, or of any amendments thereto; or under the provisions of sections 4281 to 4289, inclusive, of the Revised Statutes of the United States, or of any amendments thereto; or under the provisions of any other enactment for the time being in force relating to the limitation of the liability of the owners of seagoing vessels.

Section 9, 46 U.S.C. App. § 1309

Nothing contained in this Act shall be construed as permitting a common carrier by water to discriminate between competing shippers similarly placed in time and circumstances, either (a) with respect to their right to demand and receive bills of lading subject to the provisions of this Act; or (b) when issuing contracts of carriage, either in the surrender of any of the carrier's rights and immunities or in the increase of any of the carrier's responsibilities and liabilities pursuant to section 5 of this Act; or (c) in any other way prohibited by the Shipping Act, 1916, the Shipping Act of 1984, or of any amendments thereto.

Section 11, 46 U.S.C. App. § 1310

Where under the customs of any trade the weight of any goods in bulk inserted in the contract of carriage is a weight ascertained or accepted by a third party other than a carrier or the shipper, and the fact that the weight is so ascertained or accepted is stated in the contract of carriage, then, notwithstanding anything in this Act, the contract of carriage shall not be deemed to be prima facie evidence against the carriers of the receipt of goods of the weight so inserted in the contract of carriage, and the accuracy thereof at the time of shipment shall not be deemed to have been guaranteed by the shipper.

Section 13, 46 U.S.C. App. § 1312

This Act shall apply to all contracts that include the carriage of goods by sea covering transportation to or from the United States. As used in this Act, the term "United States" includes its districts, territories, and possessions. Every contract of carriage covering a shipment from a port of the United States shall contain a statement that it shall have effect subject to the provisions of this Act.

Sec. 2. This Act shall take effect ninety days after the date of its approval. Cases in which the goods were received by a carrier prior to the effective date of this Act shall be governed by the law that would have applied but for the passage of this Act.

Sec. 3. This Act may be cited as the "Carriage of Goods by Sea Act of 1996."

INDEX